Marie Curie

by
Sean M. Grady

Lucent Books, P.O. Box 289011, San Diego, CA 92198-9011

These and other titles are included in The Importance Of biography series:

Benjamin Franklin
Chief Joseph
Christopher Columbus
Marie Curie
Galileo Galilei
Richard M. Nixon
Jackie Robinson
H.G. Wells

Library of Congress Cataloging-in-Publication Data

Grady, Sean M., 1965–
    Marie Curie / by Sean M. Grady
    p. cm.—(The Importance of)
    Includes bibliographical references and index.
Summary: Examines the life of the Polish-born scientist who, with her husband Pierre, was awarded a 1903 Nobel Prize for discovering radioactivity.
    ISBN 1-56006-033-6 (acid-free paper)
    1. Curie, Marie, 1867–1934—Juvenile literature. 2. Chemists—Poland—Biography—Juvenile literature. [1. Marie Curie, 1867–1934. 2. Chemists.]
I. Title. II. Series.
QD22.C8G73   1992
540'.92—dc20   92-21031
[B]   CIP
                                                              AC

Contents

Foreword

THE IMPORTANCE OF biography series deals with individuals who have made a unique contribution to history. The editors of the series have deliberately chosen to cast a wide net and include people from all fields of endeavor. Individuals from politics, music, art, literature, philosophy, science, sports, and religion are all represented. In addition, the editors did not restrict the series to individuals whose accomplishments have helped change the course of history. Of necessity, this criterion would have eliminated many whose contribution was great, though limited. Charles Darwin, for example, was responsible for radically altering the scientific view of the natural history of the world. His achievements continue to impact the study of science today. Others, such as Chief Joseph of the Nez Percé, played a pivotal role in the history of their own people. While Joseph's influence does not extend much beyond the Nez Percé, his nonviolent resistance to white expansion and his continuing role in protecting his tribe and his homeland remain an inspiration to all.

These biographies are more than factual chronicles. Each volume attempts to emphasize an individual's contributions both in his or her own time and for posterity. For example, the voyages of Christopher Columbus opened the way to European colonization of the New World. Unquestionably, his encounter with the New World brought monumental changes to both Europe and the Americas in his day. Today, however, the broader impact of Columbus's voyages is being critically scrutinized. *Christopher Columbus,* as well as every biography in The Importance Of series, includes and evaluates the most recent scholarship available on each subject.

Each author includes a wide variety of primary and secondary source quotations to document and substantiate his or her work. All quotes are footnoted to show readers exactly how and where biographers derive their information, as well as provide stepping stones to further research. These quotations enliven the text by giving readers eyewitness views of the life and times of each individual covered in The Importance Of series.

Finally, each volume is enhanced by photographs, bibliographies, chronologies, and comprehensive indexes. For both the casual reader and the student engaged in research, The Importance Of biographies will be a fascinating adventure into the lives of people who have helped shape humanity's past, present, and will continue to shape its future.

Important Dates in the Life of Marie Curie

Curie is born as Manya Sklodowska in Warsaw, Poland. — **1867**

1886 — Begins work as a governess in the rural Polish town of Szczuki.

Enrolls in the University of Paris as Mademoiselle Marie Sklodowska. — **1891**

1893 — Receives her *licence és sciences physiques,* the French equivalent of a master's degree in physics.

Employed by France's Society for the Encouragement of National Industry to study the magnetism of steels; receives her degree in mathematics and meets Pierre Curie. — **1894**

1895 — Marries Pierre Curie.

1897 — Begins her investigation of "Becquerel rays" as her doctoral thesis; Pierre joins in her work.

Announces with Pierre the discovery of polonium and radium; begins her four-year effort to prepare a pure sample of radium. — **1898**

1903 — Receives her doctorate in physics from the University of Paris; Marie and Pierre Curie and Henri Becquerel share the Nobel Prize in physics for the discovery of radioactivity.

Pierre is killed when a horse-drawn wagon runs over him in a busy Paris street; the University of Paris selects Marie Curie to succeed her husband as professor of physics, and she becomes the University's first female professor. — **1906**

1911 — France's Academy of Sciences refuses to grant Curie membership because she is a woman; she receives the Nobel Prize in chemistry for the discovery of radium and polonium; she is accused of having a romantic affair with Paul Langevin, a married colleague.

World War I begins; Curie begins setting up a network of portable and hospital-based X-ray machines to treat wounded soldiers. — **1914**

1918 — World War I ends; Curie officially opens the Radium Institute of the University of Paris.

Makes her first visit to the United States to raise money for the Radium Institute. — **1921**

1934 — Curie's older daughter, Irène, and son-in-law, Frédéric Joliot, discover artificial radioactivity; Curie dies of leukemia caused by radiation poisoning.

The Accomplishments of Marie Curie

Marie Curie was a true scientific pioneer. She was one of the first scientists to investigate radioactivity, and she was *the* first scientist to recognize that radioactivity is the result of changes in the atoms of an element. In addition, she discovered the radioactive elements radium and polonium, which exist only in microscopic quantities in nature.

Marie Curie contributed enormously to the fields of chemistry and physics, in spite of social barriers to women scientists.

Altogether, Marie's work helped open the field of atomic physics for study. And because of her research and achievements, she won two Nobel Prizes—one in physics in 1903 and one in chemistry in 1911. Today, only three people, including Marie Curie, have achieved this distinction.

But the effects of Marie Curie's work went beyond the laboratory. She began her scientific career in 1891 as a student at the University of Paris, when women scientists were virtually nonexistent. Women simply were not encouraged to study science, and they were often actively discouraged from studying it by universities and by society. Nevertheless, Marie Curie followed her dream of doing scientific research, and her achievements have inspired women scientists around the world.

Science in the 1890s

Marie Curie made her most famous discoveries in the late 1890s, during a period of worldwide scientific progress. Scientists were beginning to figure out the forces that hold the universe together. Every year, discoveries were made that showed flaws in the old ideas of how nature worked. This rapid progress and increase in knowledge happened in all scientific fields, from physics to chemistry to biology.

The discoveries made and the philosophies developed during this time still influence our lives today. British physicist Alex Keller, in his 1983 book, *The Infancy of Atomic Physics,* summed up the effect this period had on the world:

> For more than half a century we have been living on the intellectual muscle built up during the twenty years that ended with the . . . First World War. Our art and music, our politics—our physical science, and above all our scientific technologies are working out ideas born at the turn of the century. In a few short years old assumptions were challenged and overthrown in every field. . . . In science, at least, it was a time of renaissance, renewal, adventure, which it was hoped would make the twentieth century even more glorious than the nineteenth.[1]

Marie Curie had a great deal to do with overthrowing one of these assumptions. Until the 1890s, scientists thought that atoms were the smallest particles of matter. Larger chunks of matter—houses, trees, people—were made up of atoms that somehow managed to stick together. Scientists did not know how these atoms were connected or how they stayed together. But they believed that there was no way to divide an atom into smaller parts.

Marie Curie's pioneering research provided the first major challenge to this theory. The elements she studied convinced her that atoms could break down into smaller parts. By studying radioactivity, Marie discovered that the atoms of radioactive substances were shooting out tiny pieces of themselves. This action

could only mean that there were bits of matter smaller than atoms. Other scientists investigated Marie's theory. Before long, many scientists were using Marie's theory of radioactivity to redevelop models of how atoms were constructed.

Studying Science in a Man's World

Marie Curie was instrumental in challenging another idea: that women were not capable of original scientific thought. Male scientists and university directors in Marie's time believed that women's minds were arranged for "soft" tasks like caring for a home and children. Scientific thought,

Curie did much of her later work in this Paris laboratory.

Starting her teaching career in the 1730s, Laura Bassi was the first female physics professor in a European university.

scientists set. But these women formed an extreme minority in the male-dominated world of science. And women who did receive their degrees were forced to take positions as assistants to male scientists.

Marie Curie, like other women in science, fought this mind-set throughout her career. She was accused of building her career on the work of her husband, Pierre, and other male colleagues. Some scientists said that she merely acted as a technician, percolating chemicals while Pierre made the truly great discoveries. And despite the fact that she was awarded two Nobel Prizes, Marie was never admitted to the French Academy of Sciences because she was a woman.

But her passion for her studies and her belief that being a woman was irrelevant to

American astronomer Maria Mitchell discovered a new comet in 1847, and was elected to the American Academy of Arts and Sciences the following year.

which involved unlocking the secrets of the universe, was thought to be a "hard" task. It was judged to be more suited for the supposedly superior and more flexible male mind.

Women scientists before Marie Curie had failed to overcome this assumption. The first female physics professor in a European university, Laura Bassi, began teaching in the 1730s. In the United States, amateur astronomer Maria Mitchell discovered a new comet in 1847 and became the first woman elected to the American Academy of Arts and Sciences in 1848. More women followed, or tried to follow, in the paths these two and a few other

her pursuit of science allowed Marie Curie to press on with her research. In 1903, she became the first woman in France to earn a doctorate in science. Three years later, she was appointed a professor of physics by the University of Paris. She was the first woman in France to hold such a position.

Later in her life, Marie defined the basic unit of measurement for radioactivity—the curie—and prepared a standard sample of radium by which all other samples were measured. With the aid of her daughter Irène and a few assistants, she set up a network of X-ray examination stations throughout France during World War I. For many doctors, these stations were their first chance to use X rays to diagnose injuries. And Marie almost single-handedly created France's Radium Institute, which became a leading center for the study of radioactivity.

Marie Curie's life was not a series of successes, however. She suffered many personal hardships, including the accidental death of her husband when she was thirty-eight. Her reputation and her health were nearly destroyed by allegations that she had a relationship with a married colleague. And, worst of all, she suffered burns and other problems caused by her continual exposure to high levels of radioactivity. Yet her determination and her dedication allowed her to pursue her research, despite these setbacks.

Chapter 1
Polish Childhood, Parisian Scholarship

Marie Curie was born in Warsaw, Poland, on November 7, 1867, to a family of Polish intellectuals. Named Manya, or Maria, Sklodowska, she was the youngest of the family's five children. Her mother, Bronislawa Boguska Sklodowska, was the director of a school for girls. Her father, Vladislav Sklodowski, was a physics and mathematics professor at one of Warsaw's gymnasiums, which are schools similar to American high schools.

In the eighteenth century, Poland had been invaded by and divided among Russia, Austria, and Prussia (a former German kingdom that is now part of Germany). During the nineteenth century, Warsaw, where the Sklodowskis lived, was in an area of the country that was under Russian control.

The czar, or emperor, of Russia, Alexander II, wanted to destroy all traces of the native Polish culture. In the past, Poles seeking freedom had rebelled against their Russian rulers. With Poland's sense of nationality destroyed, the czar thought, the country would not seek independence in the future. The Polish language was all but forbidden; only Russian could be used in public and official life.

The Sklodowski children, (left to right) Zosia, Hela, Manya, Jozeph, and Bronya.

The Russian government ran all schools in Poland, except for a few elementary schools. Any attempt by Poles to educate their own children beyond elementary school was illegal. But few Polish teachers were willing to teach in Russian-controlled schools. As a result, most secondary school classes were taught by Russians.

Russians also filled all the high-paying positions in Warsaw's government. Because his family was Polish, Vladislav Sklodowski was forced to take low-paying jobs that offered little hope of promotion. Madame Sklodowska quit her job to take care of her children when her second child, Bronya, was born. Because of these hardships, Marie and her family had to cut costs to survive on her father's small salary.

Alexander II, the czar of Russia, sought to absorb Poland into Russia by trying to eliminate the Polish language and culture.

Russian Oppression

Marie carried the memory of Russia's cruel treatment of the Polish people, and especially its effect on her schooling, all her life:

> All instruction was given in Russian, by Russian professors, who, being hostile to the Polish nation, treated their pupils as enemies. Men of moral and intellectual distinction could scarcely agree to teach in schools where an alien [Russian] attitude was forced upon them. So what the pupils were taught was of questionable value, and the moral atmosphere was altogether unbearable. . . . Amidst these hostilities they lost all the joy of life, and precocious feelings of distrust and indignation weighed upon their childhood.[2]

Russia's attempt to break the spirit of the Polish people had the opposite effect, however. Many Poles were determined to hold on to their culture at all costs. They began to teach the Polish language and history in defiance of Russian law. In this atmosphere, Marie was inspired to gain a university education and also to teach. Her father, who wanted all his children to pursue university degrees, encouraged her desire, though he worried about how she would pay for it. She did not know exactly what subject she would study—she was drawn to both physics and literature. But Marie knew where she would study—not in one of the official Russian-controlled universities but in a foreign school where she would not be fed anti-Polish propaganda. Marie hoped that once she had her degree, she could become part of a movement to educate Poles about their oppression and to free Poland from Russian control.

Keep to Yourself

Vladislav Sklodowski, Marie's father, did a great deal to dampen Marie's patriotic fervor to free Poland from Russian control when she was a student in Paris. One time, she wrote to him describing a party she had attended, dressed as a personification of "Poland breaking her bonds." Author Robert Reid in his biography Marie Curie *quotes what her father wrote back.*

"I deplore your taking such active part in the organisation of this theatrical representation. Even though it be a thing done in all innocence it attracts attention to its organisers, and you certainly know that there are persons in Paris who inspect your behaviour with the greatest care, who take notes of the names of those who are in the forefront and who send information about them here, to be used as might be useful. This can be the source of great annoyance, and even forbid such persons access to certain professions. Thus, those who wish to earn their bread in Warsaw in the future without being exposed to various dangers, [must] remain unknown. Events such as concerts, balls, etc. are described by certain correspondents for newspapers, who mention names. It would be a great grief to me if your name were mentioned one day. This is why, in my previous letters, I have made a few criticisms, and have begged you to keep to yourself as much as possible."

Professor Vladislav Sklodowski, Marie's father, was very concerned about the futures of his children. He is pictured here with his daughters, (from left to right) Marie, Bronya, and Hela.

There were other hardships Marie had to overcome besides Russian oppression and her family's poverty. Both her oldest sister, Zosia, and her mother died from tuberculosis, a lung disease. Zosia died when Marie was only nine years old; her mother's death came two years later. Their deaths left Marie with a lifelong dread of disease. Because tuberculosis, which slowly consumes its victims, was thought to be caused by the confinement of city living, Marie also developed a belief in the benefits of physical exercise, especially in the open air of the countryside.

Despite the hardships of her life in Poland, Marie excelled in her studies at the gymnasium. She was driven both by her desire for a university education and by the high standards set by her sister Bronya and brother Jozeph. Both of them had graduated at the top of their class, earning gold medals from the school for their performance. Marie matched their performance in 1883, though the physical strain forced her to spend a year in the country on vacation. When she returned to Warsaw in 1884, she began planning her university education.

Tutoring for Bronya's Education

Marie and Bronya shared a similar goal—to earn a university degree and find a job to benefit Poland. They both wanted to study at the University of Paris in France. Paris was a center of culture in the nineteenth century. The University of Paris, also known as the Sorbonne, was one of the best and oldest institutions in Europe. For Poles living under Russian control, Paris was a haven of learning and freedom. And though Russian rule was strict, some Poles were allowed to travel outside the country.

Unfortunately, the cost of living in Paris and attending the university was more than Marie and her sister could afford. Their

The University of Paris, or Sorbonne, where Marie dreamed of attending school.

Marie (left) and her sister Bronya worked to pay for each other's education at the Sorbonne.

was older, would go to Paris first and study to become a medical doctor. Marie would stay in Poland and take a job as a governess, teacher, and nursemaid for young children. Once Bronya completed her university studies and began practicing medicine, she would help pay for Marie's education.

With her gold medal and tutoring experience, Marie easily found a position with a family in the rural Polish village of Szczuki. She spent only four hours a day teaching her two pupils. For three years, from 1886 to 1889, Marie spent her spare time reading science books. She had discovered she liked the rigorous thinking that went into studying the sciences and working out mathematical problems. Marie decided that when the time came for her to go to Paris, she would register at the Sorbonne as a physics student.

When her three-year contract in Szczuki was over, Marie returned to Warsaw. For the next year, she was a governess for a wealthy family living in the city. But at the end of the year, she went back to living in her father's house. She had a lucky break when a reform school near Warsaw hired her father as its director. He finally

father was unable to help. Although the two young women tutored children for a little extra money for the family, this would not be enough to finance their education.

To solve this problem, Marie and Bronya decided to pool their resources. Bronya, who

The house in the Polish village Szczuki where Marie worked as a governess. Most of the money Marie earned was used to pay for her sister Bronya's medical training.

had enough money to pay for part of Bronya's tuition. Marie, who continued tutoring schoolchildren, was able to use her money to save for her own studies.

Secret Lessons

Marie also began conducting textbook experiments in a barely legal teaching laboratory disguised as the Museum of Industry and Agriculture. This laboratory was established by one of the many underground groups that formed throughout Poland.

Dmitry Mendeleyev developed the first periodic table of elements. One of his students was Marie's cousin Jozeph Boguski, who helped Marie learn chemistry in a clandestine Warsaw laboratory.

These groups attempted to teach forbidden knowledge to young Polish intellectuals. Both Marie and Bronya had taken part in another of these informal academies before Bronya left for Paris. Called the Floating University, it was an illegal night school with classes ranging from literature to mathematics. It was a "floating" university because its members always met in a different location.

"Like all educational processes carried on in Poland outside the Russian system it had to be done in secret," said one of Marie Curie's biographers, "and those who took a role in it did so with a real risk to themselves. The 'University' lecture halls were top-floor apartment drawing-rooms, safe from the eyes of the State police; the 'professors' included not only genuine teachers, who risked their careers, livelihoods and a winter in Siberia, but also half-qualified enthusiasts, many of them with half-developed and sometimes half-baked ideas."[3]

The laboratory Marie worked in, however, was no half-baked institution. Its director was her cousin Jozeph Boguski, and he had studied with Dmitry Mendeleyev, the Russian chemist who developed the first practical periodic table of elements. Another lab worker, who occasionally helped Marie with her work, had been a student of Robert Bunsen, a famous German chemist. Marie Curie later recalled her "great joy" at finally working in a laboratory:

> I found little time to work there, except in the evenings and on Sundays, and was generally left to myself. I tried out various experiments described in treatises on physics and chemistry, and the results were sometimes unexpected. At times I would be encouraged by a little unhoped-for success, at others I

Robert Bunsen was a famous German chemist who had taught one of the lab workers at the Floating University. The lab worker used what he had learned from Bunsen to help Marie with her work in the laboratory.

would be in the deepest despair because of accidents and failures resulting from my inexperience. But on the whole, though I was taught that the way of progress is neither swift nor easy, this first trial confirmed in me the taste for experimental research in the fields of physics and chemistry.[4]

By the fall of 1891, Marie felt she was ready to leave Warsaw for Paris. Bronya, who had earned her doctorate, invited Marie to live with her near the outskirts of Paris. Bronya had married a Polish classmate,

Casimir Dluski, in 1890 and was already a mother. She and her husband had a medical practice in an office in their second-floor apartment, where they treated their neighbors. "So it was in November, 1891, at the age of twenty-four," Marie later wrote, "that I was able to realize the dream that had been always present in my mind for several years."[5]

Studies at the Sorbonne

Manya Sklodowska changed her first name to Marie when she registered at the Sorbonne that November. At the time, admission to the Sorbonne was open to anyone who demonstrated the ability to handle university class work. Evidently, the knowledge and laboratory experience Marie had accumulated was enough to let her register as a candidate for the *licence és sciences physiques* (degree in physical sciences), roughly the equivalent of a master's degree.

But Marie soon discovered that university life would be difficult. Her private studies, despite the effort she put into them, had left her barely qualified for the Sorbonne. Marie's classmates, who had benefited from the French education system, were much more advanced. They had studied the latest discoveries in physics, chemistry, and other sciences and already had the equivalent of a modern four-year college degree. Marie, on the other hand, had the equivalent of a very good high school diploma. Though she supplemented her gymnasium work with her independent science studies, she had only a fraction of the knowledge of her classmates. Besides, much of her information came from books she found in Polish libraries and was probably out-of-date.

In addition, Marie was forced to study in a foreign language. She had studied French, one of the world's accepted languages of science, during her school days in Poland. Written French was no problem for her. But life in Poland had not given her the chance to practice speaking and listening to the language. Often, she could not understand what her professors or fellow students were saying. This problem was compounded when she ran into unfamiliar French scientific terms or phrases.

A Hermitlike Existence

In her drive to correct these problems, Marie began to lead a hermitlike life-style common to students in her day. She spent most of her free time studying in a library until closing time, then went home and studied late into the night. She moved out of her sister's house partly because it was an hour's ride in a horse-drawn carriage from the university. In addition, Bronya and Casimir were constantly taking her out for concerts and other social gatherings. To avoid these distractions, Marie moved to a place of her own.

For the next few years, Marie stayed in a series of top-floor, or garret, apartments near the Sorbonne. With no elevators in the apartment buildings, these rooms were the cheapest available. Like many students, Marie had very little money for rent, food, and other expenses. The need to conserve money outweighed the effort of having to climb six flights of stairs each day. Of course, there were other disadvantages to

Paris, around the time Marie lived there to begin her studies in physical science at the Sorbonne.

Limiting the Female Mind

In deciding upon a career in science, Marie Curie was challenging centuries of intellectual bias against women. A passage from the 1986 book Women in Science *by Marilyn Bailey Ogilvie describes the mind-set Marie had to fight.*

"At the turn of the century, although much of the world of scholarship had been opened to women, their numbers in scientific disciplines remained low. Writer Emily Hahn's adviser in the College of Engineering at the University of Wisconsin in 1926 reflected the attitude of many in scientific and technical fields. She was wasting his time and hers, he explained, for she would not get a degree.

'Why won't I get my degree?' I said.

Shorey sighed. 'The female mind,' he explained carefully and kindly, 'is incapable of grasping mechanics or higher mathematics or any of the fundamentals of mining taught in this course.'"

the garret apartments. In the summer, the apartments became sweltering furnaces as the sun beat down on the roof overhead. In the winter, they were frigid because the heat leaked out through the roof. Often, when she had used up her monthly supply of heating coal, Marie would sleep covered by all her blankets, her clothes, and occasionally a chair.

In her early Sorbonne years, Marie also established a pattern of self-denial that would be as much a plague as it was a benefit. Although her devotion to her studies gradually decreased the gap in knowledge between Marie and her classmates, she often forgot to take care of herself. Once, she collapsed from fatigue and malnutrition in the middle of a sidewalk. When her brother-in-law heard about the incident, he forced Marie to return to his home until she had recovered.

Degrees Lead to a New Job

Nevertheless, Marie succeeded in gaining her Sorbonne degree. In the summer of 1893, she took the exam for her physical sciences degree and passed, at the top of her class. Later that year, she returned to the Sorbonne to study for a *licence* in mathematics. She passed the exam for that degree in 1894, graduating with the second-highest score. She also got her first professional research job in 1894. France's Society for the Encouragement of National Industry needed a scientist to investigate the magnetic properties of steel. Marie had become known for her precise, methodical laboratory work, impressing her professors with the care and skill she displayed. With her abilities, Marie easily earned the contract for the job.

This last achievement presented a problem, however. Though she was able to do some work in one of her professor's laboratories, she soon found that she needed more space. Fortunately, Marie had written about her trouble to a friend of hers from Szczuki, who had married a physics professor named Kowalski from the University of Fribourg in Switzerland. The professor, who was on a lecturing trip to Paris, thought he might have an answer to Marie's problem. A friend of his was chief of the laboratory at a Paris technical school called the School of Industrial Physics and Chemistry, or EPCI, which is the French abbreviation of the school's name. Kowalski invited Marie to his temporary Paris home to meet his friend, Pierre Curie.

Marie went to Pierre Curie in 1894 to ask for laboratory space. The two formed an instant friendship based on similar interests and values.

Pierre Curie

The first encounter between Marie Sklodowska and Pierre Curie was a true meeting of minds. A devoted scholar, Marie believed that scientists should work solely to advance knowledge. She felt scientists should conduct their experiments and publish their results without seeking commercial rewards. "In science we should be interested in things, not persons" was a motto she lived by her entire professional life.

Pierre Curie was a true example of Marie's ideal. He was a genius who had earned his *licence és sciences* when he was only nineteen. In 1882, when he was twenty-three, he was hired by the School of Industrial Physics and Chemistry as laboratory chief. Pierre was not concerned with the fact that the school lacked the prestige of other institutions. He was satisfied that he would be able to conduct his own research, in addition to his other duties, and that was all that mattered to him.

Pierre was well known for his study of crystals. When Marie met him, his best-known work was the discovery, made while working with his brother Jacques, of piezo-electricity. This is the electric charge a crystal generates under pressure, and it was later put to use in crystal radio sets. Pierre was also known for his studies of magnetism and of the symmetry of different structures in nature, including the symmetry of the human form.

With these achievements, Pierre could have held a position with more prestige, such as a professorship at the Sorbonne. His job as laboratory chief and instructor was far below his capabilities. But Pierre hated the idea of competing for promotions or for positions at more prestigious

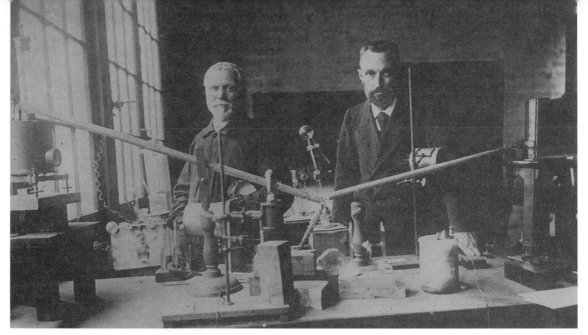
Pierre Curie with an assistant in his laboratory. He was devoted to his research, and admired the same singleminded devotion in Marie.

schools. He was even disturbed by the process for achieving doctoral degrees, in which candidates present original research to be judged by a panel of university professors. As a result, Pierre did not get his doctorate from the Sorbonne until 1895.

Pierre Curie's only complaint with his position was the lack of his own laboratory space. He often had to set up his personal experiments on tables in the school's hallways. Pierre was devoted to his research, and often lost track of his surroundings while pondering some scientific question. According to a story reported by a biographer of Marie Curie, one day a number of Pierre's students stayed late at school in order to continue a scientific discussion. Though the afternoon wore on, the little group remained in their classroom as Pierre delved deeper and deeper into his topic:

Suddenly someone noticed the clock. Another student hastily tried the door.

School was over, the building was closed, and they were locked in. Undeterred, they climbed out the second-story window and shimmied down a drainpipe running alongside, with Pierre in the lead—still talking. Such exploits, in addition to his kindliness, further endeared the soft-spoken, introspective teacher to those who worked with him and Petit (his first and only laboratory assistant at EPCI who stayed with him until he died).[6]

Pierre was not able to help Marie gain laboratory space. But the meeting had a profound effect on both of them. Marie quickly noticed the combination of dreamer and intellectual in the thirty-five-year-old scientist. Pierre, on the other hand, found Marie to have a mind as sharp as his and an intellect similar to his own. A friendship quickly grew between the two, and they often met to discuss science and other topics.

Science for Science's Sake

The idea of "pure research" is a confusing concept these days. In Marie Curie, *Robert Reid provides an idea of what the concept once meant.*

"Purity in science meant that the process of science should be carried out only with a view to the widening and deepening of knowledge. It should not be carried out with a view as to its practical application to any particular problem. If it could be applied (and as it happened there is no fundamental research which is not sooner or later applied) then so much the better for mankind, but this should not be an original aim."

A Friendship Quickly Leads to Love

Early on, Pierre realized he wanted to marry the young Polish woman. But Marie was torn between continuing her studies in Paris to gain her doctorate and teaching in Poland. To keep Marie in France, Pierre began his own courtship, one that suited both Marie's intellect and her temperament. He pointed out that if Marie stayed in France with him, she would have more opportunities for pure research. He also told her that their life together would be a life of shared research. Even when Marie visited Poland in 1894 after earning her second degree, unsure whether to stay with her father or permanently move to France, Pierre courted her through the mail.

Finally, Marie returned to Paris in September to finish her research on steel and to start work on her doctorate. She gradually became more involved with Pierre's life, even joining his parents in urging him to complete his doctorate. Pierre gave in to this joint assault, receiving his degree in March 1895. Roughly three months later, Marie in turn gave in to his request that she share his life. The two scientists were married on July 26, 1895, in a simple civil ceremony. Marie, practical and levelheaded even on her wedding day, wore a dark suit that she could use while working in the laboratory.

Chapter

2 The Discovery of Radium

Marie and Pierre Curie spent most of their married life pursuing their scientific research. In fact, Marie started on the work that made her famous less than two years after she and Pierre were wed. They did have a life outside the laboratory, however, including trips to the theater and parties at the homes of their colleagues. And they enjoyed riding the bicycles they bought just before their marriage. Each year, they

Marie and Pierre Curie in front of their home in 1906. For vacations, they often went on bicycle trips.

took a trip through the French countryside. They spent only a short time on these vacations before they felt the need to return to their lab work. The first of these trips was their honeymoon and it lasted little more than six weeks.

For the first few years after her marriage, Marie investigated the magnetism of steels for the Society for the Encouragement of National Industry. The director of EPCI, a friend of Pierre's, allowed twenty-eight-year-old Marie Curie to use the school's laboratories for her work. The fact that the scientist was also the wife of the school's laboratory chief, rather than simply an independent researcher, made the arrangement seem logical. She had to pay for her own research materials and lab time, but she was able to get free samples of steel from nearby mills. And she was able to ask Pierre, who was a known expert on magnetism, for advice during her work.

X Rays and Becquerel Rays

At the same time that Marie began her research, Wilhelm Röntgen (pronounced "rent-gen"), a German physicist, made a remarkable discovery that would affect her career. He had been experimenting with cathode-ray tubes—glass tubes containing two electric terminals in a near-perfect vacuum. When a current is sent to the terminals, the trace amounts of gas in the tube start glowing, or fluorescing. These glowing gases trace a line from the negative terminal, called the cathode, to the positive terminal, the anode. The scientist who discovered this effect, a British physicist named William Crookes, thought that the gases glowed from the effect of invisible rays. Because these rays seemed to be generated by the cathode, he called them cathode rays.

Cathode rays were a unique phenomenon when Crookes discovered them in the mid-1800s. The only things in nature that acted anything like the cathode rays were the streams of light in the atmosphere,

An aurora in the night sky glows like the gases in a cathode tube. To scientists of Marie's day, this phenomena seemed similar to the glow produced by cathode rays.

called auroras, that appear in the Northern and Southern hemispheres of the planet. Soon, physicists everywhere began examining the properties of these strange rays.

Röntgen was investigating the effects of cathode rays outside the vacuum tube itself. By the 1890s, other scientists had discovered that the rays can travel an inch or two outside the glass walls of the tube. Certain minerals placed next to the tube begin to fluoresce when hit by these rays. Röntgen was interested in finding out how thick a barrier the cathode rays could penetrate. In one of his experiments, Röntgen covered a cathode-ray tube with a hood made of thick black paper and placed a fluorescent mineral next to it.

When Röntgen switched on the tube, he noticed that a paper screen coated with a fluorescent mixture of barium, platinum, and cyanide began to glow very strongly. The amazing thing was that this screen was a couple of feet away from the tube. According to all that Röntgen knew,

Wilhelm Röntgen, the scientist who discovered X rays during his experiments with cathode tubes.

cathode rays did not have the power to travel far enough to have this effect. Yet the screen at the end of his workbench was glowing as strongly as if it were right next to an uncovered tube. Röntgen theorized that this mysterious effect must be caused by a completely different type of ray generated by the cathode tube. He began putting different materials between the tube and the screen to see if there was a way to block this effect. He found that the new rays could expose a photographic plate. He also discovered that the mysterious rays could penetrate many solid objects, including human flesh.

Röntgen gave these rays a name that reflected their mysterious, unknown nature: X rays. He spent much of the first few

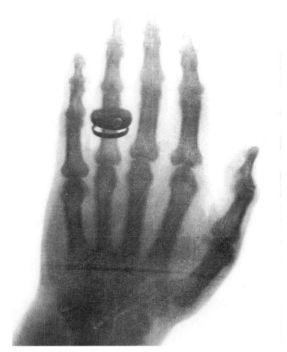

One of the first X-ray photographs taken by Röntgen after his discovery of the phenomena.

months of 1896 demonstrating X rays throughout western Europe. During one of these demonstrations, held in Paris, a physicist named Henri Becquerel had a flash of insight. X rays, he thought, might not be generated by the electrodes of the vacuum tube. Instead, they could be given off by the trace amount of gas in the tube when it becomes charged with electricity. He further theorized that minerals that glowed when exposed to sunlight might generate similar rays.

Becquerel Builds on Röntgen's Discovery

Becquerel began experimenting with different fluorescent materials—in particular,

Sir William Crookes conducts an experiment with his specially constructed cathode tube.

THE NEW ROENTGEN PHOTOGRAPHY.
"LOOK PLEASANT, PLEASE."

This cartoon from Life *magazine makes fun of Röntgen's newly discovered X-ray photography.*

with a mineral made up of potassium, sulphur, and uranium. Becquerel set a sample of the mineral in the sun for a few hours. Then, he placed the sample on a photographic plate, wrapped in black cloth to protect it from outside light. He hoped that the sun's ultraviolet rays would cause the mineral to give off rays like Röntgen's X rays, which could penetrate the cloth and expose the plate. At first, the experiment seemed to work as he had planned. But one plate had to be set aside when the sky became overcast, blocking out the sun. Becquerel put the plate, with the mineral sample still on it, in a lightproof drawer and planned to conduct the experiment later.

When the sky did not clear after a few days, however, Becquerel decided to develop the plate. Nobody knows for sure why he did this. Alex Keller suggests Becquerel had hoped "that some activity might have continued for a little while as if by phosphorescence [another form of luminescence similar to fluorescence]."[7] At most, Becquerel would have expected to see only a shadow on the plate. Instead, the outline of the mineral sample appeared more clearly than it had when it was exposed to the sun for a few hours. Becquerel repeated the experiment, letting the sample sit in the dark for a few weeks, with the same result.

This discovery was remarkable. Science at that time could not explain how a mineral could give off rays without being exposed to light or any other source of energy. X rays, at least, could be explained as a product of electricity's passage through a vacuum tube. But for a solid bit of matter to spontaneously give off this kind of energy was unheard of.

A doctor examines the chest cavity of a patient with the help of a fluoroscopic screen.

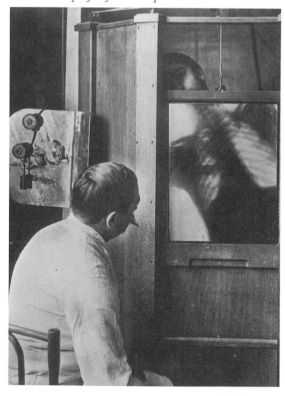

Henri Becquerel discovered that uranium samples emitted rays strong enough to leave marks on photographic plates, even when they were not exposed to an outside energy source. These rays were called Becquerel rays, to distinguish them from the much stronger X rays discovered by Röntgen.

Further experiments heightened Becquerel's interest in the phenomenon. He found that these new rays had to be coming from uranium. Minerals that did not contain uranium did not leave images on the photographic plate. Likewise, pure samples of uranium gave off more rays than mineral samples with combinations of uranium and other elements. Until Becquerel's discovery, scientists had considered uranium to be a relatively unimportant element. Its only real use was as a dye for cloth and some types of glassware. When Becquerel published his findings, he named the rays coming from uranium "uranic rays" to distinguish them from Röntgen's X rays. Other scientists called them "Becquerel rays." Becquerel rays did not, however, gain the immediate fame X rays had achieved. For one thing, they did not seem strong enough to pass through matter like X rays. Becquerel could not show any dramatic photographs of living skeletons. All he had to show were the outlines of uranium-bearing minerals. Becquerel rays were considered to be rather unimportant oddities of nature. Even their discoverer gradually lost interest in them. By the beginning of 1898, only a few scientists continued to study their effects. One of these scientists was Marie Curie.

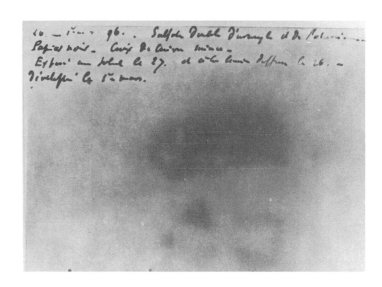

Becquerel's photographic plate, marked by the uranium sample he left on top of it.

A Perfect Subject for a Thesis

Marie Curie had been fairly busy since her marriage to Pierre. In the fall of 1896, she received a teaching certificate to help earn a little more money. The following year, she completed her research, presenting a paper on the magnetism of steels. One of her biographers described it as "over-long and not particularly original; it was, however, exceptionally thorough and showed that the young woman was as capable as any other worker in the field of many hours of sustained application at the laboratory bench with meticulous attention to her chosen problem's details."[8]

Soon after she presented her report, Marie gave birth to her first child, a daughter named Irène. The pregnancy, with its accompanying fatigue, had forced her to cut back on her laboratory work. It had also kept her from following up on her final goal of earning her doctorate. As soon as she recovered and hired someone to help clean the house and care for the baby, she returned to her search for a topic for her thesis, a long paper documenting original research that must be presented by degree candidates. As Alex Keller relates, women did not attempt such tasks in 1897:

This was the year when Cambridge [Cambridge University in England] decided by an overwhelming majority not to let women receive the university's degrees: they might study, attend lectures at the risk of puerile [childish] snubs; and despite the conviction of most lecturers that their pretty little heads must be incapable of taking in serious academic thoughts, they might even take examinations, and do well in them. But degrees—would that not frighten away male students, discourage them from going to Cambridge? Even *Nature* reports these declarations with a straight face, and apparently with approval. Paris, Berlin, and London might be more accommodating; yet there too, most found it easy to assume that the most suitable conclusion

Marie and Pierre with their daughter, Irène. After Irène's birth, Marie began to pursue her doctoral degree.

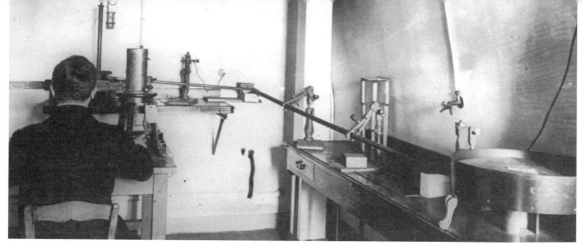

Marie used a piezo-electroscope like this one in the early stages of her search for radium. The device was invented by her husband, Pierre.

for a woman science student's career was to marry a male scientist; perhaps she could keep up with something light in her hours of leisure.[9]

But Marie Curie was determined not to let these social objections keep her from her mastery of science. Moreover, Pierre was equally determined to have his wife reach his own academic level. It was his dream that she should fully share his work, that they should conduct their experiments side by side.

A Thesis Topic

Marie decided to study Becquerel rays for her thesis topic, although how she found out about them is unclear. Her biographers suggest she came upon them through her own reading on the subject. Other historians believe that the Curies and Becquerel were at least professional acquaintances and sometimes discussed the latter scientist's discoveries. Whatever the reason, Marie and Pierre both saw the

activity of uranium as a perfect thesis subject. It was still a brand-new phenomenon that few people had researched. In fact, the only published work Marie could find was a report Becquerel made to the French Academy of Sciences in 1896. Investigating the effects of uranium would be, as Marie's younger daughter, Eve, would later write, "a leap into great adventure, into an unknown realm."[10]

Once again, the director of EPCI allowed Marie to conduct her experiments at the school. The first thing she did was to see if any other element besides uranium gave off Becquerel rays. Becquerel had found that uranium gives off a faint electric charge to the surrounding air. Marie searched for these faint charges in the air around other minerals and elements. In this search she used a device Pierre and his brother Jacques had developed: the piezoelectric quartz electrometer. Piezoelectric quartz is a rock that gives off a slight electric charge when put under pressure and that changes shape when charged by electricity. The electrometer measured the strength of electric fields by how they distorted the quartz.

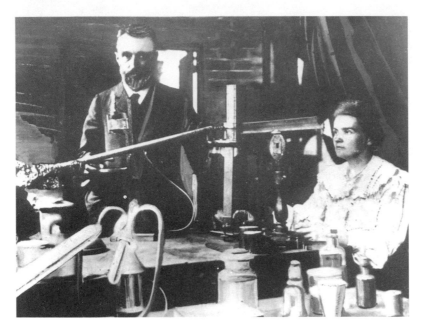

Marie and Pierre work together in the laboratory.

Marie borrowed samples of every element and mineral compound she could find and tested them in her machine. Her first success came when she tested thorium and found that it too emitted Becquerel rays. A professor who had taught Marie at the Sorbonne named Gabriel Lippmann presented a paper she wrote on the similarities of uranium and thorium rays to the French Academy of Sciences. Submitting such papers was a way for French scientists to receive recognition for an invention or a discovery. Only members of the academy could present papers for publication in *Comptes Rendus,* its professional journal. But academy members often presented papers written by nonmembers, especially by talented young scientists. Unfortunately, a German physicist named Gerhard Schmidt had made the same discovery and published the fact two weeks before Marie did. Traditionally, the credit for a new discovery goes to the first scientist to publish a report on it.

Even so, Marie's discovery proved that she was on the right track. Fortunately, Schmidt thought the uranium and thorium rays were simply weak, naturally occurring forms of X rays and stopped his research. The field of study was left wide open for Marie. And there was much work to be done. During her earlier investigation, Marie had discovered that some minerals—a uranium-bearing ore called pitchblende, in particular—were extremely active in giving off rays. Marie's analysis showed a higher level of activity than could be explained by the amount of uranium and thorium the samples contained. She later wrote:

> The activity of these minerals would have had nothing astonishing about it, if it had been in proportion to the quantities of uranium or thorium contained in them. But it was not so. Some of these minerals revealed an activity three or four times greater than that of uranium. . . . Speculating about the

Unexpected Results

The discovery of polonium and radium was an example of how scientific research can lead a scientist to completely unforeseen results. In her 1923 book, Pierre Curie, *Marie recounted how her discovery took place.*

"I had occasion to examine a certain number of minerals. A few of them showed activity; they were those containing either uranium or thorium. The activity of these minerals would have had nothing astonishing about it, if it had been in proportion to the quantities of uranium or thorium in them. But it was not so. Some of these minerals revealed an activity three or four times greater than that of uranium. . . . There must be, I thought, some unknown substance, very active, in these minerals. My husband agreed with me and I urged that we search at once for this hypothetical substance, thinking that, with joined efforts, a result would be quickly obtained. . . .

"Of course, I did not expect, even at the beginning, to find a new element in any large quantity, as the minerals had already been analyzed with some precision. At least, I thought there might be as much as one per cent of the unknown substance in the minerals. But the more we worked, the clearer we realized that the new radioactive element could exist only in quite minute proportion and that, in consequence, its activity must be very great. Would we have insisted, despite the scarcity of our means of research, if we had known the true proportion of what we were searching for, no one can tell; all that can be said now is that the constant progress of our work held us absorbed in a passionate research, while the difficulties were ever increasing."

reason for this, there seemed to be but one explanation. There must be, I thought, some unknown substance, very active, in these minerals. My husband agreed with me and I urged that we search at once for this hypothetical substance, thinking that, with joined efforts, a result would be quickly obtained.[11]

Pierre and Marie Join Forces

Pierre by this time had become intrigued by Marie's work. Interested in the possibility of finding a new element, he set aside his own work to serve as Marie's assistant. Together, they began breaking down a one-hundred-gram sample of pitchblende ore, testing its component elements for signs of activity. Aside from uranium, the two scientists found signs of activity in small amounts of the element bismuth. But bismuth, they knew, did not give off rays. Marie had tested it already.

Marie and Pierre realized that some unknown element must have chemically bonded itself to the bismuth. Over the next three months, they continued to purify their sample. Through different chemical processes, they separated more and more bismuth from the unknown element. The increasingly pure samples of the unnamed element gave off extraordinary amounts of Becquerel rays. By the end of June 1898, Marie had ray-emitting samples that were three hundred times more active than uranium.

Once again, Gabriel Lippmann presented a nonmember's paper to the Academy of Sciences. This time, the paper carried the names of both Marie and Pierre, and it announced their discovery of the new ray-emitting element. Marie had decided to call the element *polonium.* She still felt patriotism for her native Poland and had hope of its eventual freedom. She thought the element's fame would serve to focus public attention on the country's plight as well as annoy Poland's Russian rulers.

Marie Coins the Term Radioactivity

The report to the Academy of Sciences also contained a statement that many people regard as Marie Curie's greatest contribution to science. She said that the rays emitted by uranium, thorium, and polonium could not be the result of chemical reactions, which produced fluorescence, for example. The rays were emitted by the elements themselves. The emissions did not depend on heat, light, or other outside influences. These rays, Marie claimed, were the result of changes within the atoms of the elements themselves. Something about these elements made their atomic structure unstable. Because the rays were a force that radiated out from the atom, Marie called the phenomenon radioactivity. She called the elements that emitted these rays radioactive.

An even bigger discovery was to come, however. The Curies had analyzed the liquid left over when they filtered out the bismuth and polonium. This act was typical of their thorough laboratory technique. While other scientists might have discarded this liquid as waste, in the Curies' lab no material was left unexamined. In this case, the extra effort revealed that the liquid was still radioactive. But why? Analyses showed that no polonium had been left behind, and the only identifiable element was nonradioactive barium. Once again, the Curies had discovered an unknown and highly radioactive element. "After several months more of close work we were able to separate this second new substance," Marie later wrote. "In December, 1898, we could announce the discovery of this new . . . element, to which we gave the name of radium." [12]

Radium came from the Latin word *radius,* meaning "ray." Marie also had this word in mind when she coined *radioactivity.* Though the sample of radium the Curies had was small and still impure, it was nine hundred times more radioactive than uranium.

The discovery of polonium and radium both shocked and intrigued the scientific world. Some scientists refused to believe Marie's conclusion that changes were taking place in the supposedly solid atom. Sir William Crookes was one of these nonbelievers. He theorized that instead of changing atomically, radium and polonium merely tapped into some outside energy source scientists could not measure. He suggested that the two elements, which are comparatively heavy, caught hold of lighter, fast-moving molecules in the atmosphere and drained their energy. Other scientists refused to believe that radium and polonium were even elements, claiming they were simply combinations of other elements. But the majority of the world's scientists were convinced that *something* was happening to the atoms of the two elements as well as to those of uranium and

Sir William Crookes did not believe that Marie had discovered radioactivity.

thorium. Perhaps, they thought, radioactivity could be the tool they needed to examine atomic structure.

Sheer Drudgery

So far, Marie and Pierre had benefited from an incredible streak of good fortune. In less than a year and a half, they had verified that both uranium and thorium were radioactive and had discovered two new elements. Marie herself had come up with a theory of atomic behavior that would soon revolutionize the field of physics.

Normally, scientific progress is not made so quickly. It usually takes many years of experiments to bring about results like these. Biologist Keith S. Thomson, in his 1991 book *Living Fossil: The Story of the Coelacanth,* gives an excellent summation of what scientific work is like:

> Science . . . is usually not the sort of hard-edged exercise that is so glamorous to the popular press. The scientist does not carefully amass perfectly lucid arguments based on crystal-clear facts as if he or she were plucking diamonds from the bed of a stream. Instead, the facts have to be teased out gradually. Often what we need to know is only partially revealed, and we continue to add to it slowly. What we think is a *fact* may change year by year. The personality of the investigator is important in this sort of work because he or she controls not only what is studied and how it is done but, in the end, what is actually revealed.[13]

Nevertheless, Marie and Pierre had indeed plucked "diamonds from the bed of

Proving That the Atom Could Break Apart

Marie's theory that radioactivity was the result of atomic changes in an element, rather than some sort of chemical reaction, was an astounding leap of intuition. In her doctoral thesis, "Radioactive Substances," Marie presents her argument about the nature of radioactivity.

"The radio-activity of thorium and uranium compounds appears as an *atomic property*. M. Becquerel has already observed that all uranium compounds are active, and had concluded that their activity was due to the presence of the element uranium. . . . I have investigated, from this point of view, the compounds of thorium and uranium, and have taken a great many measurements of their activity under different conditions. The result of all these determinations shows the radio-activity of these substances to be decidedly an atomic property. It seems to depend upon the presence of atoms of the two elements in question, and is not influenced by any change of physical state or chemical decomposition."

A page from Marie's notebook shows her calculations of the atomic weight of radium.

a stream." Now, however, came a period of long, slow work. Radium and polonium had been discovered, but virtually the only evidence of their existence was their radioactivity. Marie and Pierre needed a pure sample of each element to prove that it existed. The only way to get these pure samples was to purify a huge amount of pitchblende in hopes of getting a tiny flake of each material.

Fortunately for the Curies, the Austrian Empire was operating a uranium extraction plant at the Bohemian uranium mine of Saint Joachimsthal. The Curies found out that there were hundreds of tons of ore wastes piled up near the plant. All the uranium had been removed from these wastes, making them excellent sources for the extraction of radium and polonium.

With the help of an Austrian geologist, Eduard Suess, who was an admirer of Pierre's, the Curies convinced the Austrian government to sell them some of the wastes. The French scientists were required to pay only for the cost of shipping the material to their lab at EPCI. Even so, the expense almost emptied their small bank account.

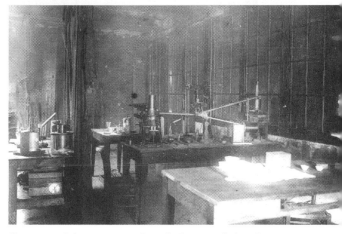

Because of the amount of work that needed to be done, Marie and Pierre required more room than they had in their small EPCI laboratory.

Terrible Working Conditions

Because of the amount of work that needed to be done, Marie and Pierre could not continue to use the old storage room as their laboratory. The only available space at the school, however, was a large wooden shed in the school's yard. It had been used as a dissecting room for medical students but was now merely a dirty, empty building. Marie knew she and

Pierre would have to make the best of a bad situation:

Its glass roof did not afford complete shelter against the rain; the heat was suffocating in summer, and the bitter cold of winter was only a little lessened by the iron stove. . . . There was no question of obtaining the needed proper apparatus in common use by chemists. We simply had some old pine-wood tables with furnaces and gas burners. We had to use the adjoining yard for those of our chemical operations that involved producing irritating gases; even then the gas often filled our shed.[14]

The Curies put up with these conditions for the next four years. Marie herself always viewed these years as the happiest and most productive of her life. In addition to their work with radium, Pierre taught classes at EPCI and Marie taught at a nearby girls' school. Some evenings, the Curies would attend a play or a party. And the couple occasionally managed to get away to the country with their daughter for a few days or weeks of bicycle travel.

The two scientists soon divided the work of purifying a sample of radium. Marie decided to take over the physical task of separating radium from the other elements. Pierre, meanwhile, conducted experiments on the radioactivity in the ever-purer samples Marie provided. Marie had decided to purify a sample of radium first. According to her data, polonium existed in smaller quantities than radium

Marie (back row, middle) with her students from a local girls' school. In addition to her research with radium, Marie had to take a teaching position to help support her family.

did. With their primitive equipment, the Curies could have spent a decade before getting measurable results. As it was, Marie did not have a sample of radium until March 1902. Even this sample was not pure radium, but radium chloride. Nevertheless, there was enough radium in the sample to verify its existence.

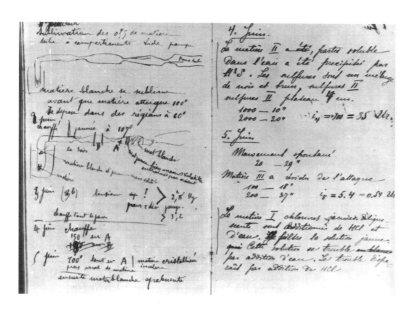

Two pages from Marie's laboratory notebook. Pierre's handwriting is mixed with hers.

Radioactivity's Effects

Aside from destroying living cells, the intense level of radioactivity emitted by radium can cause ordinary materials to glow. In her doctoral thesis, Marie describes some of the things that glow when exposed to radium, and mentions a practical use for this effect.

"A large number of bodies are capable of becoming phosphorescent or fluorescent by the action of Becquerel rays. . . . Paper, cotton, glass, etc., are all caused to fluoresce in the neighborhood of radium. . . . The diamond becomes phosphorescent under the action of radium, and may thus be distinguished from paste imitations, which have only a very faint luminosity."

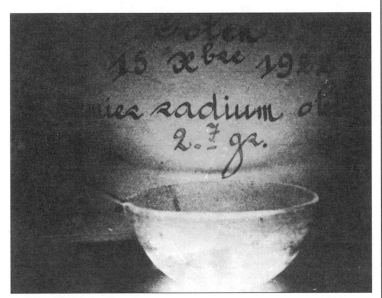

Radium glows in a laboratory dish, even in complete darkness.

"Très Honorable"

By 1902, Marie Curie had discovered, named, and—with her husband's assistance—isolated the new element radium. With that task completed, she now had to prepare her doctoral thesis on the topic for presentation at the Sorbonne. Throughout the previous four years, the Curies and Andre Debierne, a laboratory assistant, had published many papers on the activity of radium and the effects of the rays it emitted. Debierne had discovered a third radioactive element, actinium, in 1899. Now, however, Marie had to take all that information and assemble it into a single comprehensive report that would be judged by more experienced scientists. This task took Marie another year.

Marie's doctoral examination took place on June 25, 1903. Accompanying her to the Sorbonne were Pierre, his father, Marie's sister Bronya, a few scientist friends, and Marie's students from the girls' school. All knew of the years of effort Marie had put into her quest, and all expected her to sail over this final hurdle. A strong factor in Marie's favor was that, as a result of her years of work, she knew more about radioactivity than her judges did. All she had to do was defend her results.

In the biography *Madame Curie,* Marie's younger daughter, Eve, reconstructed the scene at the University of Paris that day:

The three examiners [Gabriel Lippmann, her former professor, and two other scientists known only as Professors Bouty and Moisson] in evening dress sat behind a long oak table. They took turns in asking questions of the candidate. . . . Marie answered in a gentle voice. Sometimes she traced the design of an apparatus on the blackboard with a piece of chalk. She explained the results of her research in sentences of technical dryness, with dull adjectives. But in the brains of the physicists around her . . . a "transmission" of another order took place: Marie's cold words changed into a dazzling and exciting picture: that of one of the greatest discoveries of the century.

Scientists disapprove of eloquence and comments. In confirming on Marie the rank of doctor, the judges . . . [used] in their own turn words without brilliance. . . . M. Lippmann, the president [of the examining committee], pronounced the sacred formula:

"The University of Paris accords you the title of doctor of physical science, with the mention 'très honorable.'"

When the unobtrusive applause had been stilled, he simply added in friendship, with the timid voice of an old scholar:

"And in the name of the Jury, madame, I wish to express to you all our congratulations."[15]

And congratulations were very much in order. Achieving the distinction of *très honorable,* which means "very honorable," was an additional honor. It is equivalent to the honor summa cum laude (with highest praise) and is given only to degree candidates who have performed exceptionally well. Once more, Marie had received the highest score possible.

But Marie Curie's victory was even greater. For the first time in history, a woman had received a doctorate from the University of Paris. Marie had proved that she could do the same work as any other scientist in France. And the distinction added to her doctorate showed she was equal to, if not better than, any other doctor of physical sciences the Sorbonne had produced.

3 Prizes, Poisoning, and Fame

At first, the discovery of polonium and radium had little effect on the Curies' peaceful life of science. They continued their work with only occasional interruptions from scientists who wanted more information about the discoveries published in *Comptes Rendus*. Within a few years, however, journalists began appearing at their laboratory, asking for interviews. The discovery of a new element, made on the threshold of a new century, was too good a story to pass up. By 1903, Marie's doctoral project had put the unwilling Curies in the spotlight.

Marie's work created other problems for the two scientists. For most of 1903, Marie and Pierre were ill and in pain. They both thought their problems were due to the long hours they put in at the laboratory. They knew that they were skimping on their meals, even though they made sure Irène was eating correctly. And, in Marie's case, there was an extra complication. She had become pregnant toward the beginning of the year. She was enthusiastic about having a second child, but she had to endure the added physical strain

Marie and Pierre in their garden with their daughter, Irène.

and exhaustion, and this made her work more difficult.

In August, after Marie passed her final exam, she and Pierre decided to take one of their bicycle trips through rural France. Marie left for their intended vacation spot—the Ile d'Oleron near the port of Saint-Trojan—to find a place to stay between journeys. She had gone on a similar trip just before Irène was born, so she did not fear for her unborn child on this trip. But this time, something went drastically wrong. During her travels around the island, Marie suddenly went into premature labor. The child, a girl, died soon after birth.

The Prize

If August was the low point of 1903 for the Curies, then November was their high point. In the middle of that month, they received a telegram from the Royal Swedish Academy in Stockholm. The telegram said simply that Marie, Pierre, and Henri Becquerel had been awarded the Nobel Prize in physics for the discovery of radioactivity.

The Nobel Prize awards were established in 1895 by Alfred Nobel, the Swedish chemist who invented dynamite. The invention had made Nobel rich, but his conscience was uneasy at the thought of profiting from this instrument of destruction. He decided to create an institution that would benefit humanity and the cause of peace by giving out awards to recognize the greatest accomplishments in chemistry, physics, medicine, and literature, as well as the most notable work done for the cause of peace, in a particular year. (An award for economics was created

later.) The Nobel Foundation started giving out awards in 1901.

Although 1903 was only the third year the awards were made, they were already regarded as a great honor. Much of the regard for the awards stemmed from the fact that the winners were selected by prominent members of Sweden's scientific, medical, and literary communities. The first physics prize had gone to Wilhelm Röntgen for his discovery of X rays. Though he had made the discovery in 1895, Röntgen had "contributed most materially to the benefit of mankind," the attribute Nobel wished to reward.

With their award, Becquerel and the Curies were immediately identified as

Alfred Nobel established the Nobel Foundation to award prizes to those who have "contributed most materially to the benefit of mankind."

three of the world's greatest scientists. Soon after the awards ceremony on December 10, 1903, Great Britain's Royal Society gave the Curies its own award, the Davy Medal. Marie and Pierre, however, treated both awards as matters of little importance. While they appreciated the recognition of their work, they were neither impressed by nor accustomed to these honors. Writing to her brother Jozeph the day after the awards ceremony, Marie spent two paragraphs talking about family matters before mentioning the two awards:

> My husband has been to London to receive the Davy Medal which has been given us. I did not go with him for fear of fatigue.
>
> We have been given half of the Nobel Prize. I do not know exactly what that represents; I believe it is about seventy thousand francs. For us, it is a huge sum. I don't know when we shall get the money, perhaps only when we go to Stockholm. We are obliged to lecture there during the six months following December 10.
>
> We did not go to the ceremonial meeting because it was too complicated to arrange. I did not feel strong enough to undertake such a long journey (forty-eight hours without stopping, and more if one stops along the way) in such an inclement season, in a cold country, and without being able to stay there more than three or four days. We could not, without great difficulty, interrupt our courses for a long period.[16]

As the letter mentioned, Marie and Pierre were too tired from their work and Marie's miscarriage to receive their medals and cash awards in person. Instead, the

The front and back of the medal which is awarded to winners of the Nobel Prize. Marie and Pierre Curie received the prize along with Henri Becquerel in 1903.

French ambassador to Sweden accepted the award on their behalf. Pierre himself was barely strong enough to sail across the English Channel to accept the Davy Medal.

Overwhelmed by Fame

The Curies had to face a fatigue of a different sort after news of the Nobel Prize was published. Even though Henri Becquerel was awarded half of the physics prize, the Curies got virtually all of the publicity.

Newspaper reporters, as well as the world in general, were captivated by the idea of the husband-and-wife science team that had discovered radium. Their years of hardship, working in their shed-laboratory at EPCI, made for especially good newspaper stories. Marie and Pierre found themselves portrayed as nearly godlike figures who had bestowed the miracle of radium upon their fellow human beings.

The Curies found all of this utterly ridiculous and, even worse, considered it a severe infringement on their research time. They had been forced to talk to reporters who invaded their EPCI laboratory in 1902, soon after they announced Marie's isolation of radium. The Curies had been able to turn their unwanted guests away after answering a few of their questions.

But in 1903, they were famous. Reporters were not willing to leave after a brief interview with Pierre or Marie. They wanted the couple to be available whenever they, the reporters, wanted to speak with them. Soon, the Curies' assistants were turning away journalists at the doors of EPCI, the Sorbonne, and Marie's girls' school so the couple could continue working. Reporters even stopped by the couple's home in Paris, collecting information for articles on Irène.

Pierre often complained to his friends about the sudden fame the Nobel Prize had created. In one letter, filled with irony, he detailed the social hysteria that had invaded his life:

You have seen this sudden fad for radium. This has brought us all the advantages of a moment of popularity; we have been pursued by the journalists and photographers of every country on earth; they have even gone so

Marie and Pierre in their laboratory. The couple became famous after they won the Nobel Prize.

far as to reproduce my daughter's conversation with her nurse and to describe the black-and-white cat we have at home. Then we have received letters and visits from all the eccentrics, from all the unappreciated inventors. . . . We have had a large number of requests for money. Last of all, collectors of autographs, snobs, society people and sometimes even scientists come to see us in the magnificent establishment in the Rue Lhomond [the street in front of their EPCI shack] which you know. With all of this, there is not a moment of tranquility in the laboratory. . . . I can feel myself being overwhelmed by brute stupidity.[17]

Pierre also complained about the great number of requests he kept receiving from scientific societies, newspapers, and other groups: "People ask me for articles and

A Scientist in Her Own Right

As early as 1902, some scientists claimed that Marie's discoveries actually had been made by Pierre but that he had let his wife take the credit. In the conclusion of her doctoral thesis, Marie made sure her examiners knew that she had done her own work.

"I will define, in conclusion, the part I have personally taken in the researches upon radio-active bodies.

"I have investigated the radio-activity of uranium compounds. I have examined other bodies for the existence of radio-activity, and found the property to be possessed by thorium compounds. I have made clear the atomic character of the radio-activity of the compounds of uranium and thorium.

"I have conducted a research upon radio-active substances other than uranium and thorium. . . . I discovered that certain minerals possess activity which is not to be accounted for by their content of uranium and thorium. . . .

"In conjunction with M. Curie, and subsequently with MM. Curie and Bemont, I was able to extract from pitchblende two strongly radio-active bodies—polonium and radium.

"I have been continuously engaged upon chemical examination and preparation of these substances. . . . The work has proved *that radium is a new chemical element.* Thus the new method of investigating new chemical elements, established by M. Curie and myself, based upon radio-activity, is fully justified. . . .

"Our researches upon the new radio-active bodies have given rise to a scientific movement, and have been the starting-point of numerous researches in connection with the new radio-active substances, and with the investigation of the radiation of the known radio-active bodies."

lectures, and after a few years are passed, the very persons who make these demands will be astonished to see that we have not accomplished any work."[18]

Marie was equally, if not more, discouraged by the intrusion upon her professional and private life. The point of scientific research, she felt, was to bring knowledge to humanity, not to bring glory to the scientists. Her lifelong motto—"In science we must be interested in things, not persons"—was up against its severest test. At times, she would deny being Marie Curie simply to get away from journalists who tried to interview her in public.

Fame Leads to a New Position for Pierre

This unwanted fame did have a few benefits, however. For years, Pierre had been trying to get a higher-ranking position with access to a proper laboratory. Until he and Marie won their share of the Nobel Prize, however, his efforts had failed, precisely because of his hatred of competition and his inability to promote his accomplishments.

In 1900, Pierre was hired as an assistant professor at the Sorbonne's School of Physics, Chemistry, and Natural Sciences.

Marie with her daughter Irène and her new baby, Eve.

Known generally as the PCN, this school mainly taught future physicians. Even so, the job did not include access to a laboratory. Pierre was forced to keep his EPCI job so he and Marie could continue their radium work. But in 1903, with the Curies' newfound fame, Pierre and his supporters had the leverage they needed to force the Sorbonne to admit him as a full professor.

Pierre's biggest supporter in 1904 was a colleague from the Academy of Sciences, known only as L. Liard, who was named rector of the university. Liard convinced the government's Chamber of Deputies (the equivalent of the U.S. Congress) to order the university to create a position especially for Pierre. The position included a small laboratory that was to be built in the PCN courtyard. Best of all, the university also hired Marie to work as Pierre's laboratory chief. The two appointments came at the right time for the Curie family. In 1904, Marie gave birth to her second daughter, Eve.

Poisoned by Radiation

These successes were marred by the fact that Marie and Pierre were suffering from increasing fatigue. Pierre was often immobilized by attacks of rheumatism in his legs. Marie, though she was never bedridden, also grew weaker and thinner. She blamed her long hours of lab work for her ill health. And both scientists shared a similar ailment—their hands were burned and continually swollen. They knew this last condition was caused by the radiation given off by the radium they had purified.

Early on in their purification of radium, Marie and Pierre had noticed a curious fact about the new element's radioactivity. After handling a very active sample of radium and bismuth, their hands developed what looked like burns. Pierre decided to investigate this phenomenon, exposing his own skin to a concentrated dose of radiation:

> After the action of the rays, the skin became red over a surface of six square centimeters; the appearance was that of a burn, but the skin was not painful, or barely so. At the end of several days the redness, without growing larger, began to increase in intensity; on the twentieth day it formed scabs, and then a wound which was dressed with bandages; on the forty-second day the epidermis [the skin's outer layer] began to form again on the edges, working toward the center, and fifty-two days after the action of the rays there is still a surface of one square centimeter in the condition of a wound, which assumed a grayish appearance indicating deeper mortification [cellular damage or death].
>
> I may add that Mme. Curie, in carrying a few centigrams of very active matter in a little sealed tube, received analogous burns, even though the little

Henri Becquerel, a fellow researcher of the Curies', was burned on his chest when he carried a sample of radium in his vest pocket.

tube was enclosed in a thin metallic box. One action lasting less than half an hour, in particular, produced a red spot at the end of fifteen days, which left a blister similar to that of a superficial burn and took fifteen days to cure. . . .

> Besides these lively effects, we have had various effects on our hands during researches made with very active products. The hands have a general tendency toward desquamation [peeling of the skin]; the extremities of the fingers which have held tubes or capsules containing very active products become hard and sometimes very painful; with one of us, the inflamation of the extremities of the fingers lasted about a fortnight and ended by the scaling of the skin, but their painful sensitiveness had not completely disappeared at the end of two months.[19]

Exposure to high doses of radiation causes burns similar to this one. Marie and Pierre Curie often suffered from burns because they handled highly radioactive substances.

In her biography of Marie, Eve Curie described how her mother gave Henri Becquerel a small sample of radium in a glass tube. Becquerel carried the sample in his vest and, like the Curies, received a small burn. "Astonished and angry, he hurried to tell them about his mishap and the exploits of their terrible child. He declared, by way of conclusion: 'I love this radium, but I've got a grudge against it!'"[20]

Even though the Curies knew radioactivity was dangerous in high doses, they either did not know or would not admit that it was the cause of their persistent ill health. But modern scientists and historians consider Marie and Pierre two of the earliest victims of radiation sickness.

Radiation Sickness

Radiation sickness is a combination of diseases caused by long-term exposure to radioactivity. A brief exposure to low levels of radiation may not cause any severe damage to one's body. But the effects of radiation become more severe with repeated exposure. Radium is one of the most radioactive elements found in nature. By purifying the uranium wastes they got from the Austrian government, the Curies were exposing themselves to increasingly higher and more deadly levels of radiation. They were breathing in air contaminated with radioactive particles. Their burned and peeling hands, their chronic fatigue, Pierre's rheumatism, and even Marie's miscarriage—all these ailments are now known to be symptoms of radiation poisoning.

No one truly knows why Marie and Pierre did not try to protect themselves from these excessive exposures. Even as early as 1901, scientists knew about these rays and the materials that could block their effects. Maybe the Curies were too stubborn in their disregard for their own comfort while they pursued "pure research." Curiously, in later years, Marie would require her assistants to take precautions against exposure to radiation, even though she ignored those same rules.

Marie and Pierre were just two of the scientists working with radium who were beginning to sound the alarm about the element's dangers. At the time, though, the world was not ready to hear warnings about the new element. Radium was the greatest discovery of the age. And the citizens of the world were eager to see what new marvels its rays would illuminate.

4 Heralding the Twentieth Century

The discovery of radium and Marie's work on radioactivity had an incredible effect on the scientific community and the world. The Curies' research had overturned a long-held belief that atoms were unbreakable bits of matter. Scientists around the world had to abandon their assumptions about the way the universe worked. They began studying how elements could spontaneously generate energy in the form of radiation. And they began asking what happened to the atoms after they gave off their rays.

Radioactivity and Physics

One of the most notable early attempts to answer this question took place in 1900. Two British scientists—Ernest Rutherford, a physicist, and Frederick Soddy, a chemist—were studying the element thorium at Canada's McGill University. Thorium, when it decays, gives off a radioactive gas. (Radium gives off a similar gas, called radon. At the time, these gases were referred to as emanations of a particular element, or simply "emanations.") Rutherford and Soddy decided to experiment with the emanation of thorium. The two scientists attempted to capture the

emanation in one of several chemicals to see how the gas differed from solid thorium. Alex Keller described their experiment:

> In their main apparatus, a current of air passed over their thorium compound,

The discovery of radioactivity inspired Lord Ernest Rutherford to conduct research into atomic physics.

and then drove the emanation . . . into an ionization chamber, so . . . its radiations could be measured. Soddy inserted in the passage various acids and other chemical reagents which ought to have absorbed whatever gas it was. Yet they failed completely—the emanation passed on into the chamber unimpaired.[21]

This was an unexpected result. If the emanation were truly a gaseous form of solid thorium, it should have reacted with the chemicals Soddy had planted to absorb it. Yet the emanation had passed by these traps, acting like gases such as argon or helium, which do not interact with other chemicals. Keller reported:

Frederick Soddy worked with Rutherford during his early research into the nature of atoms.

Jean Perrin suggested the first model of an atom. He described tiny particles, or electrons, circling a larger mass, or nucleus.

Soddy was amazed. . . . He turned to his partner and exclaimed, "Rutherford, this is transmutation; the thorium is disintegrating and transmuting itself into an argon gas." Rutherford was determined not to get too excited just yet—"For Mike's sake, Soddy," he replied, "don't call it transmutation. They'll have our heads off as alchemists."[22]

Further examinations of radioactive elements confirmed Marie's theory of the atomic origin of radioactivity. In turn, examinations of how this activity took place led to the development of a whole new field of study—atomic physics. Physicists began using radioactive particles as a means of studying how the atom was put together. The electrical charge given off by radioactive materials suggested that electrons might have something to do with the process of radioactivity. Scientists knew that electrons existed, but did not know that they were a part of the atom itself. Perhaps, scientists began to think, electrons were smaller than atoms, and even were a part of the structure of atoms. In 1901, a French physicist named Jean Perrin described how the atom might be constructed. In his model, electrons were tiny particles with a negative electrical charge that circled another mass called the nucleus in the center of the atom, much like planets orbiting the sun.

By 1911, Rutherford, now working at Cambridge University, and two assistants thought they found the proof of this model. In their experiment, they aimed a stream of radioactive particles at a thin sheet of gold. Rutherford used gold because it could be rolled into sheets thin enough for particles to pass through yet sturdy enough not to tear. Some of the particles passed through the sheet, but others bounced back. Rutherford concluded that every reflected particle had hit the nucleus of a gold atom.

Radium and Medicine

Radioactivity was not just a tool for physics experiments. One of the first uses of radium outside the laboratory was as a treatment for cancer. Since burns caused by radium were eventually replaced by healthy skin, doctors wondered if radium's rays could burn out cancerous human tissue.

Cancer is simply the out-of-control growth of body cells. Cancer starts when one or more cells begin producing malformed copies of themselves. These malformed cells produce others, gradually creating a mass of cells that threatens to destroy healthy tissue and ultimately a person's life. This disease, which can strike any part of the body, has been a major cause of death for most of human history.

Radium's Role in Uncovering the Atom's Mysteries

In September 1934, the journal Scientific Monthly *described how radium had opened up the field of atomic physics.*

"Theoretically, the importance to science of the discovery and isolation of radium is great because radium has played an extensive part in the growth of knowledge of the internal structure of atoms in general. The discovery of polonium and radium led to the modern analyses of . . . the spontaneous transformations of the radioactive bodies."

Alexander Graham Bell was one of the first to suggest radiation treatment for cancer victims. He theorized that a small sample of radium would burn out the cancer in the patient's body, and the diseased tissue would be replaced by new, healthy flesh.

With radium, however, scientists and physicians saw a possible cure for this fatal disease. Alexander Graham Bell, who had taken an interest in the new element, proposed a way to use radium medically:

> There is no reason why a tiny fragment of radium sealed up in a fine glass tube should not be inserted into the very heart of a cancer, thus acting directly upon the diseased material.[23]

This and other techniques were tried. Historian Catherine Caufield, writing about the history of radiation exposures, chronicled some of the ways radium was used in medical treatments:

> In the early days doctors simply strapped flat containers of radium on to the surface of whatever part of the body they wanted to treat. To reach deeper injuries, they injected radium chloride intravenously [into the vein] or slipped small capsules into natural body cavities. That technique often resulted in severe burns—for doctor and patient. Before the First World War, Dr John Hall-Edwards, a pioneer radiologist from Birmingham, England, treated a young girl who was suffering from tuberculosis of the skin with a radium source that he had wedged into the end of a bamboo pole. Andie Clerk, who witnessed the operation as a friend of the girl's family, recalled many years later that 'He touched the skin with it very carefully, but it wasn't effective, rather defective. It made her slightly out of her mind, though I believe she got that back in later years. He was handling something which he knew was dangerous but didn't know to what extent. A few years later he lost both his hands as a result of contact with it.' Hall-Edwards said of his radiation injuries that 'the pain experienced cannot be expressed in words.'[24]

Despite catastrophes like these, physicians were able to treat other patients with varying degrees of success. One technique they used was similar to the method Alexander Graham Bell proposed. According to writer David Wilson, in this procedure, a small piece of radium, or another radioactive source, was "enclosed in glass tubes which were then enclosed in platinum needles which could be inserted surgically into the outer, growing edges of tumors."[25] This method literally baked the cancer cells to death with radioactivity. The glass tubes were then withdrawn, allowing healthy skin to replace the dead tumor.

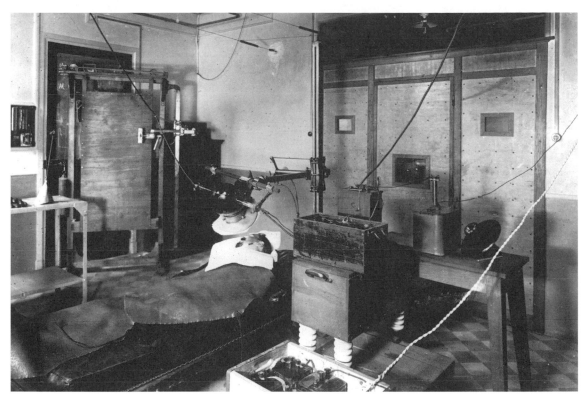

A patient receives radiation treatment for cancer.

A later method used a more manageable source of radiation—radon. Physicians developed a way of enclosing small amounts of this gas in hollow gold pellets. These pellets were surgically implanted in a patient's tumor. The radiation immediately began killing the cancer cells. The pellets did not have to be removed because radon decays into a nonradioactive form of lead within a week or two.

These techniques became known as radiation therapy throughout the world, except in France. There, the treatments were named after Marie and Pierre and were called *Curietherapy*. By refining these early techniques, doctors developed the procedures that are used today. Treatment with radiation or radioactive elements—in some cases combined with chemical injections (chemotherapy)—has cured many cancers once thought untreatable.

The Radium Industry and Popular Reaction

The use of radium as a tool of medicine soon created a large demand for this incredibly rare substance. To meet this need, many governments and private entrepreneurs with nearby uranium mines developed their own radium-processing plants. They were aided in their efforts by the Curies themselves. For a short time, Marie and Pierre were the

Radium as Fertilizer

A Scientific American article published in November 1982 reports the various ways in which radium was used.

"Not content with healing the human body, the purveyors of radium sought to sell radium-bearing fertilizers on the premise that they would increase plant growth. The fertilizers were tailings [wastes] from the radium-extraction process, in some cases mixed with ordinary fertilizer. In spite of disclaimers from the Bureau of Soils of the Department of Agriculture it appears the 'radioactive manures' were applied to soils in the U.S., Canada and France. . . .

"Other industrial applications relied on the ability of a radium source to ionize air and thereby dissipate a static charge. In the late 1920s radium static suppressors were employed in a Russian factory where rubber-coated fabric was manufactured to lessen the hazard of sparking and the ignition of flammable vapors. By the mid-1930s there was limited production in the U.S. of rayon fabric in which small quantities of radium were incorporated to reduce what television commercials now call 'static cling.'"

only people in the world who knew how to purify radium. If they had wanted to, they could have kept all rights to the process of extracting radium. They then could have sold licenses to scientists and companies who wanted to process the metal.

But the two scientists felt it would be wrong to patent or copyright their procedure for extracting radium, even though they were facing a life of continued poverty, made more difficult by the cost of raising Irène and Eve. Selling licenses would have meant a more comfortable life, but to restrict access to such an important scientific find went against their principles. As a result, the Curies sent details of their method to anyone who asked for it.

A New Industry

A French company, Central Chemical Products, was one of the first private radium mills. Starting in 1902, it purified radium for the Academy of Sciences and, therefore, did not operate for a profit. Other companies soon began producing radium in order to make money, however, creating a market for uranium ores. The Austrian government stopped selling its

Marie Curie in her laboratory. Her discovery of radium became the catalyst for scientific research into atomic physics, and for research into practical uses for radioactivity.

pitchblende wastes to the Curies or anyone else in 1903. Instead, it set up its own radium refinery. Over the next thirty years, uranium ores were located and mined in Colorado, near Canada's Great Bear Lake, in Portugal and Northern Europe, in the Belgian Congo of southern Africa, and elsewhere around the world. These ores were processed throughout the United States, Europe, and Russia, as well as in Australia.

Before long, radium and other radioactive elements found their way into general use. Local newspaper reporters had been writing stories about radium since the Curies announced its discovery in 1898. At that time, the articles focused mainly on the fact that a woman scientist working in a shed in Paris was preparing a sample of a previously unknown element. With the award of the Nobel Prize, worldwide publicity of radium promoted the many benefits of this new form of energy. Radium's very existence was called a miracle. Its magical rays, which came from the heart of the element itself, were the light that would lead humanity into the twentieth century.

This publicity generated a near-hysterical enthusiasm for radium in the general public. Although a gram of the element could cost as much as $200,000, some far-thinking business people began looking for ways to capitalize on its fame. Some of the ways in which radium was used—or at least was advertised as being used—seem absurd now. People bought bottled-water dispensers with filters that contained very small amounts of radium. The radioactive water supposedly cured attacks of "gout, rheumatism, arthritis," various aches and pains, diabetes, and even hardening of the arteries.

Health spas around the world began advertising that the water in their hot springs contained natural radioactivity. Bathing in this water, they claimed, rejuvenated tired muscles and helped energize the blood. Many spas also carved underground caves where their guests could sit and breathe in the supposedly health-restoring radon gas the springs gave off.

Other products capitalized on the public's ignorance of scientific matters in order to get customers to part with their money. One such product was a hearing aid

Radium Scams

Consumer goods that supposedly contained radium were everywhere during the first third of the twentieth century. In its November 1982 issue, Scientific American *reported that the U.S. government eventually had to take action against people making fraudulent claims about radium.*

"The unfounded medicinal claims for radium eventually led to government action and warnings, including the following press release issued in 1926 by the Bureau of Chemistry of the Department of Agriculture:

"'The products analyzed for content of radium included hair tonics, suppositories, bath compounds, tissue cremes, tonic tablets, face powders, ointments, mouth washes, demulcents [soothing creams], opiates [sleeping compounds], ophthalmic solutions [eyewashes], healing pads and other preparations. . . . Only 5 percent of the products analyzed and claimed to be radioactive contained radium in sufficient quantities to render them entitled to consideration as therapeutic agents and then only in certain very limited conditions. . . . Highly exaggerated therapeutic claims obviously designed to mislead the purchaser are being made for many of the products which contain little or no radium. One of the samples examined consisted of a short glass rod coated on one end with a yellow substance and enclosed in a glass bulb. The bulb is designed to be hung over the bed and according to the claims of the inventor causes dispersion of "all thoughts and worry about work and troubles, and brings contentment, satisfaction and body comfort that soon result in peaceful, restful sleep.""'

The radioactivity of the radium in these uranium ore samples can make some minerals glow in the dark. This property prompted many manufacturers to develop radium-based paints that were used on watches and other products.

that supposedly contained the ingredient "hearium." This "element," so the manufacturers claimed, emitted rays that cured deafness. Products made with the legitimate element radium offered equally outlandish results, such as a cure for insanity or the elimination of bad breath.[26]

In addition to the many legitimate and fraudulent medical uses of the element,

radium was used in the first glow-in-the-dark paints. These paints contained small amounts of radium and zinc sulfide, which glows when exposed to radium. By World War I, radium paint was being used in rifle sights, airplane instruments, and watch faces. Roulette wheels and balls were coated with this paint for the amusement of casino patrons, who could gamble with the lights turned off. Once, Marie and Pierre were contacted by an American dancer who wanted to know how she could make a glowing, radium-coated costume. Though the Curies told her that the cost and effort involved would make the project impossible, the dancer and the two scientists became good friends.

This contact and a few others were the only positive results the Curies received from the worldwide radium fad. The two scientists still had to contend with hordes of admirers, journalists, and other invaders who took up more of their valuable lab time. All that they wished was to have some time to themselves so Pierre could develop his class at the Sorbonne and Marie could continue her work in his lab.

5 Life After Pierre

The years Marie and Pierre spent in their shed-laboratory were bliss compared to 1904 and 1905. In addition to being hounded by celebrity seekers, they were sought out by members of the mainstream Parisian scientific community. Pierre suffered more than Marie as a result of their new notoriety. He genuinely hated being an object of public acclaim. Even so, he was forced to make himself a public figure. His Sorbonne laboratory was still not adequate for his and Marie's needs. But he lacked the professional influence that would give him an edge in asking for more space. In the end, the only solution Pierre saw was to apply for membership in the Academy of Sciences.

Pierre had applied for membership once before, in 1902. Despite his abhorrence of personal honors, he had given into pressure from his friends and campaigned for a seat at the academy. Membership was granted by election, whenever a spot was open, to one of several candidates who had applied. Each candidate was required to prove that he or she was worthy of the honor of admission. Unfortunately, Pierre's overwhelming humility made him trivialize his accomplishments, and he lost the election.

In 1905, Pierre again gave in to his friends and submitted a second application.

This time, he was told, he would be guaranteed a victory. As a Nobel Prize winner and a professor at the Sorbonne, Pierre had more than enough credentials for admission. Still, his election was close, and it took a runoff vote between Pierre and another physicist to confirm Pierre as the academy's newest member.

Pierre's research and professorship qualified him for a seat in the prestigious Academy of Sciences in 1905.

Soon after his election that July, Pierre regretted his decision. The image-conscious scientists who made up the academy were not, to Pierre's thinking, the students of "pure research" scientists should be. "I went to the institute on Monday, but I must really say I don't know what I was doing there," Pierre wrote to his friend Georges Gouy on October 6. "I have nothing to do with any of the members, and the interest of the meetings is null. I feel very clearly that these circles are not mine." A few weeks later, Pierre again complained, "I have not yet discovered what is the use of the Academy."[27]

Marie's work, fortunately, kept her from the same pressures Pierre had to face. She was busy both with her studies of radioactivity and with the new, though small, laboratory the Sorbonne had given Pierre. On top of these academic duties, the Curies also had their children, Irène and Eve, to care for. Even with their combined Sorbonne salaries, Pierre and Marie could not meet their expenses and buy the extra equipment Pierre's laboratory budget did not cover. Marie had to keep her job teaching science at the girls' school near Paris—a job she enjoyed but that kept her from her family and her research. For the near future, though, it seemed that the two scientists would be stuck with this arrangement.

On Her Own

For Marie and Pierre, the future lasted until April 19, 1906. After lunch with an association of university science professors, Pierre headed toward the Academy of Sciences. While he was crossing a busy street,

Even after winning the Nobel Prize, Marie had to keep her teaching position at the girls' school in Sevres. She is pictured here with some of her students.

the rue Dauphine, he was run over and killed by a horse-drawn wagon carrying a load of uniforms. The accident happened too fast for the wagon driver to stop in time. Pierre had stepped out from behind a horse-drawn cart without checking to see if the street was clear. His father, Eugene Curie, was living with Marie and Pierre at the time. When old Dr. Curie was told about Pierre's death, his reaction was, "What was he dreaming of this time?"[28]

Pierre's death almost destroyed Marie. Not only had she lost her husband but also a fellow scientist she deeply respected and a good friend. She hid her grief as best as she could in public. Even during Pierre's funeral, she did not cry. But her sister Bronya and Pierre's brother, Jacques, could see how distraught she was. It was as

Despite her deep grief at Pierre's death, Marie continued her research.

humblest servants, who adored him: I have never seen sincerer or more harrowing tears than those shed by his laboratory attendants at the news of his sudden decease.[29]

Despite her grief, and with Jacques's insistence, Marie soon returned to her laboratory. Jacques knew his sister-in-law well and believed that forcing her back into the lab would help her recover from her loss. Pierre, too, had insisted that their work continue even if one of them died: "Whatever happens, even if one should become like a body without a soul, still one must always work." At first, she was barely able to touch her instruments or finish an experiment. Only a few short weeks after the funeral, though, she was busy with her continued research into radium and polonium.

if Marie had been replaced by a robot. She kept her emotions inside, breaking into tears only a few times before and after Pierre's funeral. Later, it was discovered that she had kept a diary in which she wrote letters to Pierre's departed spirit.

The sense of loss Marie and her family felt was echoed by scientists and governments around the world. William Kelvin, a noted British physicist and a longtime friend and admirer of the Curies, traveled to be with Marie as soon as he heard of Pierre's death. The feelings Pierre had stirred among his colleagues were summed up by Charles Cheveneau, one of Pierre's laboratory assistants:

> Some of us had developed a true cult for him. For me he was, after my own family, one of the men I loved most; such had been the great and delicate affection with which he knew how to surround his [lab assistants]. And his immense kindness extended even to his

Irène and Eve, the Curies' daughters, became the focus of Marie's life after their father died.

Eugene Curie, Pierre's father, with Irène. After his son's death, old Dr. Curie volunteered to take care of his granddaughters while Marie worked in the laboratory.

An Uncertain Future

Marie's biggest worries were how she would raise her daughters and what the future of Pierre's laboratory would be. Fortunately, Marie did not have to worry for long. Pierre's father, Dr. Eugene Curie agreed to care for the girls while Marie worked. He stayed with the family when they moved from their Paris town house to a house in Sceaux, a suburb of Paris.

The fate of the laboratory was settled on May 13. Some of Marie's closest friends had been urging the Faculty of Sciences to name her as Pierre's replacement as professor of physics. At the time, and especially in France, this was a radical request. In the history of France, a woman had never been named as a university professor. But the lobbying by Marie's supporters, combined with Marie's credentials and the public acclaim for the widow of Pierre Curie, was enough to alter tradition. The faculty named Marie Curie assistant professor, with a guaranteed promotion to full professor in 1908.

Normally, a historic offer such as this would have pleased any woman scientist. But the offer was not made under normal circumstances. Marie received her appointment less than a month after Pierre's funeral, hardly enough time to get over the shock of his death. Instead of celebrating her achievement, Marie felt that the congratulations she received were idiotic.

In addition, Marie loathed having to lecture before huge crowds. Her feelings probably stemmed from her Warsaw childhood, when she had to recite lessons during frequent surprise visits by Russian school inspectors. Nevertheless, being a professor of physics required her to overcome her fears in order to teach her classes. The worst lecture was the first one, held at 1:30 P.M. on November 5. The lecture hall was packed with newspaper reporters, scientists, and members of Parisian society, leaving little room for Marie's legitimate students. Eve Curie later recreated the scene:

> At one twenty-five the noise of conversation grew heavy. There were whisperings and questions; necks were craned so as not to miss any part of Mme. Curie's entrance. All those present had the same thought: what would be the new professor's first words—the first

words of the only woman the Sorbonne had ever admitted among its masters? Would she thank the Minister, thank the university? Would she speak of Pierre Curie? Yes, undoubtedly: the custom was to begin by pronouncing a eulogy of one's predecessor. But in this case the predecessor was a husband, a working companion. What a strong 'situation'! The moment was thrilling, unique. . . .

Half-past one. . . . The door at the back opened, and Marie Curie walked to the chair in a storm of applause. She inclined her head. It was a dry little movement intended as a salute. Standing, with her hands strongly holding onto the long table laden with apparatus, Marie waited for the ovation to cease. It ceased suddenly: before this pale woman, who was trying to compose her face, an unknown emotion silenced the crowd that had come for the show.

Marie stared straight ahead of her and said:

"When one considers the progress that has been made in physics in the past ten years, one is surprised at the advance that has taken place in our ideas concerning electricity and matter. . . ."

Mme. Curie had resumed the course at the precise sentence where Pierre Curie had left it. . . . In the same firm, almost monotonous voice, the scientist gave her lesson that day straight to the end. She spoke of the new theories on the structure of electricity, on atomic disintegration, on radioactive substances. Having reached the end of the arid exposition without flinching, she retired by the little door as rapidly as she had come in.[30]

William Kelvin traveled to be with Marie as soon as he heard the news of Pierre's death.

With those words, Marie ensured that the work Pierre had devoted the last years of his life to would be continued. But she never forgave France's scientific community for keeping Pierre from fulfilling his intellectual promise:

For the admirable gift of himself, and for the magnificent service he renders humanity, what reward does our society offer the scientist? Have these servants of an idea the necessary means of work? Have they an assured existence, sheltered from care? The example of Pierre Curie, and of others, shows that they have none of these things; and that more often, before they can secure possible working conditions, they have to exhaust their youth and their powers in daily anxieties.[31]

With the first lecture over, Marie was ready to advance toward the next goal that confronted her. Some scientists still doubted that radium was a separate element and considered it an altered form of an existing one. William Kelvin, for one, theorized that radium might simply be a radioactive compound of helium. Marie had based her calculations proving radium an element on radium chloride, not pure radium. Though most scientists accepted radium's existence as fact, Marie herself was plagued by the idea that her work could be in jeopardy. Separating pure samples of radium and of polonium became her major work for the next four years.

Andrew Carnegie was impressed by Marie Curie and her work. He established a scholarship fund at the Sorbonne named after her and her husband. The fund enabled her to develop a group of students who would continue her research into radioactivity.

A Period of Recovery

Between 1906 and 1910, Marie made great progress in her efforts to rebuild her life. Her professional work did not produce the astounding successes of her early experiments with radioactivity. She was obsessed with the detailed—and, some biographers suggest—essentially pointless task of collecting a pure sample of radium. Even so, in 1910 she succeeded, proving for the last time that her work was valid.

At the same time, Marie had begun to take advantage of her international fame. Her public image—she was known as a "celebrated widow" and as the "radium woman"—gave her a great deal of power in dealing with her colleagues. She became aware of this fame in 1906, shortly after delivering her first lecture. American industrial tycoon Andrew Carnegie had introduced himself to Marie during a trip to Paris. During their encounter, he developed a deep respect for her work and her personality. He demonstrated his regard by establishing a scholarship fund for Sorbonne science students, entitled the Curies Foundation, to honor both the famous Marie Curie and her late husband. This gift supplied Marie with students who later formed the core of French scientists devoted to researching atomic physics.

Marie was building a reputation as a forceful and stubborn person to work with. Her students adored her and her methods, giving her the nickname La Patronne (The Patroness). But her coworkers and other scientists dreaded having to confront her powerful will. If Marie felt a certain procedure had to be done a certain way, it was almost impossible to change her mind. A classic example of this

The laboratory of the Pasteur Institute. The institute became interested in radiation therapy, and pledged funds to pay for half of the Radium Institute, so that Marie could continue research in that area.

happened in 1910, during a physics conference in Brussels, Belgium.

One of the goals of the conference was to develop a standard unit for the measurement of radioactivity so that the output of radium, uranium, and other materials could be calculated. The scientists in charge of directing the discussion thought they could make their task easier by calling the measurement the "curie." They thought giving Marie this honor would make her less likely to argue over how to define the standard. Marie, however, said that if the measurement were named after her, it should be defined by her. At times, she left the discussions, pleading illness due to her work. Given that she was exposing herself to higher doses of radiation than before, her pleas of fatigue and nausea sound reasonable. However, many of the other scientists at the conference suspected her of simply avoiding arguments she did not want to hear. In the end, she got her way.

Using Her Reputation to Advance Her Cause

Marie Curie's reputation and fame had its advantages in Paris, as well. Soon after she had adjusted to her new academic role, Marie began pressuring the Sorbonne to build a laboratory devoted to the study of radioactivity. The Radium Institute, as it was to be called, had been a dream of hers and Pierre's since 1904. The small laboratory provided by the Sorbonne was inadequate for the work Marie envisioned. She spent months trying to convince the university administration to pay for a better one. The Curies Foundation funds meant that the institute's staff was already accounted for. As an added bonus, the Pasteur Institute, France's leading medical research group, was interested in studying the growing field of radiation therapy. Having the two research groups working together would be a logical combination.

The Pasteur Institute pledged funds to build half of the new Radium Institute so that its scientists could conduct experiments in *Curietherapy*.

But the University of Paris balked at having to pay more for scientific research than it absolutely had to. Perhaps its directors thought that the facilities they had provided were enough. Marie had made her fame with work she had done in her EPCI shed; the Sorbonne's laboratory was far better than that. Still, for Marie, it was not enough. In 1908, she threatened to leave the Sorbonne and take a position with the Pasteur Institute. Her threat shocked the university into giving in to her wishes. Better to pay for a new laboratory, they thought, than to lose the woman who discovered radium.

Cooperative Education

Marie's private life was not nearly as complicated as her professional life. Still, she applied the same thorough methods to

After Pierre's death, Marie was concerned for the intellectual and physical well-being of her children.

raising Irène and Eve that she applied to her laboratory work. Her main concern was for their intellectual and physical well-being. She strongly disagreed with the common method of teaching children, confining them inside with their teacher and schoolbooks for a full day. Instead, she felt that spending too much time in the classroom hindered a child's ability to learn.

With this idea in mind, Marie formed an informal system of instruction, very much like the Floating University of Warsaw. She gathered together colleagues from the Sorbonne and friends from the intellectual community to teach the subjects they knew best. Their children studied along with the young Curies. Like the Floating University students, the children went to a different instructor each day. Marie taught them basic principles of science; Edouard Chavannes, a professor of Chinese language, taught them about world cultures and arts; others taught them music, art, French history, and other subjects. This system, which its members simply called "the cooperative," lasted for about three years. It ended when the instructors became too busy with their own work and the children had to begin the regular class work that would take them into a university.

The "Assault" on the Academy

Marie's scientific work had earned her membership in scientific societies around the world. There had been no such honor from France, however. Marie had refused the only honor France had offered her, the Legion of Honor medal. Pierre had been offered the same award in 1903, after

Marie refused the only honor France had offered her, the Legion of Honor medal.

Paris. She was also an expert on radioactivity, an accomplished physicist and physical chemist, and one of France's most beloved scientists.

There was, however, a deep feeling among many of the academy members that women did not belong in their group. In addition, they disliked Marie's forceful behavior. They might have excused it as the sign of an aggressive, typically argumentative male scientist. But Marie was a woman, and her lack of appropriate feminine submission must have been unacceptable to the academy scientists. Also, Marie's fame had created resentment in many of those scientists who had not achieved her popularity, despite decades of work.

losing his first bid for the Academy of Sciences. He had refused, partly from his opposition to awards of any sort. Marie felt the same way and made the same response. But her friends were determined that she should be honored in the country she had come to call home.

The only way to give Marie the honor she deserved was to have her admitted to the Academy of Sciences. In January 1911, the academy held an election for a seat that had opened after the death of one of its members. Marie's friends convinced her that election to the academy would benefit her efforts to gain funds and supplies for her laboratory. And with her credentials, Marie's election seemed to be a certainty. Unlike Pierre when he first applied, Marie was both a Nobel laureate and a full professor at the University of

Author George Sand was denied admission to the Academie Française because she was a woman. This tradition also excluded Marie Curie from the Academy of Sciences.

Artist Rosa Bonheur was not allowed to join the Academy of Fine Arts because she was a woman.

Worst of all, there was a tradition of not admitting women to any of the French academies. The famous writer George Sand had been refused admission to the Academie Française; painter Rosa Bonheur had been turned away from the Academy of Fine Arts. Even the Academy of Sciences had turned away a previous female applicant, the mathematician Sophie Germaine. When the election was held on January 23, Marie lost by two votes.

Ironically, Marie's opponent, Edouard Branly, paid her a higher compliment than the academy could have by admitting her. Some of Marie's supporters asked Branly, as a demonstration of chivalry, to put aside his candidacy until another seat was available. Branly refused. Replying to the request, Branly said:

> Madame Curie presents herself to me as a woman of science and therefore as my equal. I have no need to know anything about her except her achievements. It is not a question of gallantry in these circumstances.[32]

Branly's treatment of Marie as a scientist, rather than as a woman, was in itself a victory, though it is not known if Marie heard about his comment.

The Langevin Affair

Marie never again applied for membership to the Academy of Sciences. Indeed, it was nearly a decade before she even submitted articles, through friends who were members, to the academy's professional journal. But there was no time to spend brooding over her mistreatment. Marie was preparing the International Radium Standard that was to bear her name. She also attended the increasing number of scientific conferences that were being held

Edouard Branly, a physician and chemist, was admitted to the Academy of Sciences instead of Marie Curie.

Max Planck was one of the scientists involved in the frequent conferences held to discuss the rapidly expanding field of atomic physics.

to discuss the latest findings in the new field of atomic physics. In addition to Marie Curie, these conferences featured prominent scientists like Ernest Rutherford, Max Planck, and Albert Einstein.

Among the other French delegates at these conferences was Paul Langevin, Pierre's successor at the School of Industrial Physics and Chemistry. A close friend of the Curies before Pierre's death, Langevin in 1911 was assistant director of the school. Paul and his wife, Jeanne, were children of working class families. But unlike Paul, Jeanne had never received more than a basic education. They had grown apart, each developing interests that the other did not appreciate. Paul often said that she did not understand his need for and his love of research. She berated him

for not accepting one of the many industrial positions he was offered, which would have paid him more than his EPCI work.

Paul Langevin confided his problems to Marie. They shared an interest based on their scientific work. And Langevin— though five years younger than Marie— raised her spirits as only Pierre had been able to do. They began spending a great deal of time together. Some of Marie's biographers and friends think the two might have developed a romantic attachment. Others think that while their actions were suspicious, they had merely developed a deep friendship built on the years they had known each other.

Whatever the truth, Jeanne Langevin became jealous. In November 1911, she filed for divorce and told a newspaper

Marie's close friendship with scientist Paul Langevin ended when his wife accused them of having an affair.

reporter that the two scientists had been romantically involved for more than a year. Reputable newspapers played down the story, presenting the charge as unreasonable. Madame Curie, they said, could never be guilty of breaking up a marriage. But the Paris tabloids put the accusation on the front page, with headlines like "Romance in the Laboratory."

News of the scandal reached Marie while she was attending a physics conference in Belgium. She immediately wrote to the leading newspapers of Paris to deny Jeanne Langevin's story. But the scandal was too good for the tabloids to drop. The newspapers that had supported her rejection by the Academy of Sciences now printed demands that the "husband-stealing foreigner" leave France and return to Poland. Some of the members of France's scientific community, including the head of the Sorbonne's physics department, echoed these demands. But Marie's friends, including the department head's daughter, rallied to her side and began fighting back at her attackers.

The public outcry over the scandal soon reached a point of hysteria. Antifeminists, French nationalists, and other radical figures began writing and speaking out against the "Polish home-wrecker." Marie and her daughters had to flee from hostile crowds that began surrounding her home. They spent the next few weeks sheltered in a friend's house in Paris.

Marie Wins a Second Nobel Prize

Ironically, while the scandal was breaking in Paris, the Royal Swedish Academy had decided to award Marie the 1911 Nobel Prize in chemistry. This was a great honor. Marie was the first person ever to win two awards. There have been three other double-laureates since: John Bardeen, who shared the physics prize in 1956 and 1972; Linus Pauling, who won the chemistry prize in 1954 and the peace prize in 1962; and Frederick Sanger, who won the chemistry prize in 1958 and 1980.

Marie became the first person to win two Nobel Prizes when she won the prize for chemistry in 1911.

Some scientists and other observers think the award was an attempt by the Royal Swedish Academy to shame France's Academy of Sciences for the way it had treated Marie. The award was made for the discovery of radium and polonium and for the chemical isolation of pure radium. Technically, the award was valid because Marie had recently prepared a sample of pure radium as the international standard. But the discovery and initial isolation of the two radioactive elements had been made before 1903.

However, the committee made use of a loophole in the Nobel Foundation's rules. No award had been given for the discovery of radium—the 1903 physics prize was for the discovery of radioactivity—making Marie's work eligible for the chemistry prize. And without a doubt, Marie Curie deserved the prize.

Though Marie was weakened by her fight against the scandal, she attended the awards ceremony and delivered her mandatory lecture in early December. When she returned to Paris, though, she collapsed with a high fever and kidney problems as well as severe depression. Bronya committed Marie to a private clinic until her fever broke. Soon after, Paul and Jeanne Langevin settled their divorce out of court. The thing Marie had feared most was having her name tied to a messy divorce hearing. The coverage of the scandal had already exposed her private life. Being branded an adulteress in court would have ruined her. Even so, she and Langevin could not continue whatever relationship they had. In order to bury the scandal, they could see each other only as scientists in the laboratory or in other professional surroundings.

It took Marie nearly a full year to recover from the ordeals of 1911. She spent much of the time recuperating in England, at a seashore house rented by a friend, British physicist Herta Ayerton. For most of the year, Marie would not accept mail addressed to her as Madame Curie; she felt she had brought deep shame upon the name of Pierre's family. She used the name Madame Sklodowska instead. By September, however, Marie was ready to return to work and to resume her married name.

6 X Rays at the Front

By December 1912, Marie was back at work in her Sorbonne laboratory and pushing for the completion of the Radium Institute. Throughout 1913 and the first half of 1914, she devoted her time to her classes, her research, and to overseeing the construction of the institute.

The Radium Institute was almost ready to open by July 1914. The complex had been completed except for some bookshelves in a few offices. The garden in the court between the Curie laboratories and those of the Pasteur Institute was coming into bloom. Finally, Marie could continue her research alongside a staff she had trained with funding from the Andrew Carnegie Foundation. Finally, Marie could conduct her research in a laboratory she

The completed Radium Institute was almost ready to open when World War I broke out, interrupting research.

had helped design, with a staff she had trained. No more begging for lab space, no more making do with whatever was available. It seemed that the dream she and Pierre once shared was finally going to come true.

A Call to Arms

But the dream was cruelly interrupted by one of the twentieth century's great nightmares. On June 28, Archduke Francis Ferdinand of the Austro-Hungarian Empire was assassinated in the Bosnian town of Sarajevo. (Bosnia, at the time of the assassination was an independent state.) Austria-Hungary had recently taken over Bosnia, and an underground resistance movement had built up against the country's new masters.

Unfortunately, the assassin struck at a time when nationalistic fervor was increasing throughout Europe. The major powers, especially Germany and France, were looking for an excuse to go to war with each other. The death of the archduke set off a chain reaction of troop mobilizations and declarations of war in Russia, Turkey, Belgium, Great Britain, and other countries.

French soldiers leave for the front lines.

The assassination of Archduke Francis Ferdinand in Sarajevo on June 28, 1914, sparked the First World War.

The "war to end all wars," later called World War I, had begun.

When the French Ministry of War called up all able-bodied men to fight, Marie's Radium Institute was stripped of all but one of its staff. Most French citizens were confident the war would be over soon. Marie, however, realized that the conflict would end only after many years and after countless lives had been lost. She knew the institute would have to wait years before it could officially open.

Soon after the war began, German troops crossed through Belgium and into France. Fortunately, Irène and Eve were vacationing along the seacoast of Brittany far away from the front line of battle. With the girls safe, Marie's greatest fear was that her gram of radium would fall into German hands. She could not imagine a greater tragedy now than to see her entire

German soldiers aim at the enemy from well-protected trenches on the Belgian front. The German army advanced on France and occupied Paris.

German troops bombed the beautiful cathedral at Rheims, and Marie Curie feared that they would also destroy the Radium Institute.

supply of the element carried away to Berlin. With her limited finances and the onset of war, she might not be able to replace this loss.

There was a real danger that German troops would occupy Paris within a few months. The French government had already moved from Paris to the town of Bordeaux in southwestern France. Marie joined the migration, carrying her radium supply in a sealed lead box.

When Marie reached the town, however, she deposited the radium in a bank vault and caught a troop train back to Paris. Though the radium was safe from German hands, the Radium Institute was not. Biographer Rosalynd Pflaum stated:

> The thought of leaving Pierre's dream that was now immortalized in bricks and mortar never crossed Marie's mind. The Germans had already bombed the cathedral at Rheims, a medieval jewel, in an act of wanton vandalism, and she may have reasoned they would be far less apt to plunder and desecrate the empty Radium Institute if the 'Madame' herself was there.[33]

A Free Poland

Though World War I had cost millions of lives, it brought Marie one small consolation. The effects of the war and the communist revolution of 1917 had broken the Russian Empire's grip on Poland. In her autobiographical notes to the biography Pierre Curie, *Marie describes how she felt knowing that after a century of Russian occupation, Poland was free.*

"I had lived, though I scarcely expected it, to see the reparation of more than a century of injustice that had been done to Poland, my native country, and that had kept her in slavery, her territories and people divided among her enemies. It was a deserved resurrection for the Polish nation, which showed herself faithful to her national memories during the long period of oppression, almost without hope. The dream that appeared so difficult to realize, although so dear, became a reality following the storm that swept over Europe. In these new conditions I went to Warsaw and saw my family again, after many years of separation, in the capital of free Poland. But how difficult are the conditions of life in the new Polish republic, and how complicated is the problem of reorganization after so many years of abnormal life!"

"The Little Curies"

By August, it was clear that the German advance had been halted by the French army. The halt, however, had come and was maintained at the cost of thousands of French lives and thousands more wounded. French scientists were among the troops both at the front and behind the lines, serving as regular soldiers. Unlike these scientists who could not apply their intellectual talents and professional experience, Marie sought ways to use her knowledge to help France's war effort.

She soon hit upon a brilliant idea. Röntgen's X rays, the discovery that had led to her own work, had been used in medical experiments almost from the day they were discovered to see inside the human body. In the United States alone, thousands of medical X-ray photographs had located bullets and broken bones. This still-new tool of medicine could save countless lives, Marie figured, by helping treat the casualties of France's battlefields.

Though she had no direct experience with X-ray equipment, Marie had lectured on X rays many times and understood how they worked. By August and September, the worst of the French wounded were being treated in the hospitals of Paris. Therefore, Marie asked the French government and military leaders to let her coordinate a citywide X-ray network. Marie later wrote:

> However, at the beginning of the war, the Military Board of Health had no organization of radiology [in other words, X-ray treatment], while the civil organization was also but little developed. Radiologic installations existed in only a small number of important hospitals, and there were only a few specialists in the large cities. The numerous new hospitals that were established all over France in the first months of the war had, as a rule, no installation for the use of X-rays.
>
> To meet this need I first gathered together all the apparatus I could find in the laboratories and stores. With this equipment I established in August and September, 1914, several stations of radiology. . . . But as they could not satisfy the needs of all the hospitals of the Paris region, I fitted up, with the help of the Red Cross, a radiologic car. It was simply a touring motor-car, arranged for the transport of a complete radiologic apparatus, together with a dynamo that . . . furnished the electric current necessary for the production of the rays. This car could come at the call of any of the hospitals, large or small, in the surroundings of Paris.[34]

The car was a success, but the demand for its services soon became more than it could handle. By October, however, many Paris citizens who had fled to the coast returned. Marie went to humanitarian aid societies that had offices in Paris, as well as to wealthy former nobles, to raise money to build more X-ray stations. She also convinced citizens and merchants to donate cars and small trucks to carry portable units, which she assembled. Soon these vehicles, dubbed *Les Petites Curies* (The Little

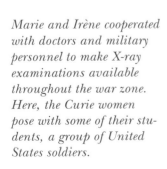

Marie and Irène cooperated with doctors and military personnel to make X-ray examinations available throughout the war zone. Here, the Curie women pose with some of their students, a group of United States soldiers.

Marie Curie in one of the motor vehicles equipped with X-ray equipment known as "The Little Curies" by the soldiers Marie treated.

Curies) by the soldiers they treated, were bringing X rays to hospitals within a mile or two of the front. Marie said:

> The motive of my starting on a journey was usually a demand from surgeons. I went with a radiologic car which I kept for my personal use. In examining the wounded in the hospital, I could gain information of the special needs of the region. When back in Paris, I got the necessary equipment to meet these needs and returned to install it myself, for very often the people on the ground could not do it. I had then to find competent persons to handle the apparatus and show them how to do it, in full detail. After a few days of hard toil, the manipulator knew enough to work the apparatus himself, and at the same time a large number of wounded had been examined. In addition, the surgeons of the region had gained an idea of the usefulness of the radiologic examination (which few of them knew at that time).[35]

Irène Joins Marie in Operating the X-Ray Wagons

Irène and Eve were among those who returned to Paris soon after the start of the war. Eve, who was ten, was sent to an elementary school where the day's lessons were given while the children rolled bandages or knitted socks for the soldiers. Irène, who was seventeen, began working with Marie in setting up the X-ray stations. Irène already had her *licence és sciences physiques* and quickly picked up the details of how to set up and run the X-ray installations. Marie had opened the Radium Institute to teach classes on operating these mobile X-ray stations, which were in constant demand. When Irène was not out near the front, she could be found teaching radiology to society matrons and chambermaids alike.

During this time, Irène also encountered the type of resistance women technicians could expect from their male counterparts

X-Raying the Victims of World War I

Before long, much of the confusion generated by the World War settled down into an orderly routine. This was especially true of the various field hospitals near the fighting fronts, where care of the wounded became an almost automatic process. In this passage, from the book The Doctor in War, *Dr. Woods Hutchinson describes the procedures he observed at one field hospital during a year-long trip to Europe in 1917.*

"Here [the wounded soldier] is met by the surgeon on duty, with his orderlies and nurses, who, with the quickness born of much practice, deftly remove his clothing and undo or expose the dressings. From the appearance of these . . . the surgeon promptly decided whether any operation is likely to be necessary or not. If not, he is borne swiftly off to the cleaning-up room of a ward, where the mud of the trenches is scraped off of him, and the blood washed out of his hair and finger-nails, and his whole body sponged and cleared and alcohol-rubbed. . . .

"If the wounded requires an operation, he is carried at once to the preparation room of the operating-theater. A very large majority do require an operation in these days of shellfire wounds when no one knows how many splinters of shell may be buried in the flesh; where every corner of the wound is packed with germs from the soil, and the tissues not merely torn and cut, but parts of them so pulped and shattered that they must be cut and cleared away in order to allow the wound to come together and heal properly. In this preparation-room, he is swiftly undressed and washed and made as nearly aseptic as possible. . . . Then the surgeon on duty carefully probes the wound with a gloved finger or sterilized forceps and gauges the extent of the injury and whether nerves, great blood vessels or joints are involved.

"If the case is an 'average' one the surgeon proceeds with the operation himself at once, but if it presents special features of difficulty or interest, he turns it over to the surgical specialist on the staff in whose province it belongs. . . . One [specialist], for instance, will have had special experience in surgery of the brain and spinal cord; another, of the abdomen; another, of the nerves; and another, of the joints."

Shattered Beings

Winston Churchill in his 1938 book The World Crisis *describes a visit to France in 1915 where he witnessed conditions similar to those Marie and her daughter Irène had to deal with during World War I.*

"More than 1,000 men suffering from every form of horrible injury, seared, torn, pierced, choking, dying, were being sorted according to their miseries into the different parts of the Convent at Merville. At the entrance, the arrival and departure of the motor ambulances, each with its four or five shattered and tortured beings, was incessant: from the back door corpses were being carried out at brief intervals to a burying party constantly at work. One room was filled to overflowing with cases not worth sending any farther, cases whose hopelessness excluded them from priority in operations. . . . An unbroken file of urgent and critical cases were passed towards the operating room, the door of which was wide open. . . . Everywhere was blood and bloody rags."

Winston Churchill, Great Britain's First Lord of Admiralty during World War I.

and learned how to work around it. As biographer Robert Reid relates:

There was a considerable resistance at that time, particularly among older doctors, to the use of X-rays as a means of diagnosis and both women during these early months of the war experienced resentment to their presence in military hospitals. Marie Curie later described how on one occasion the girl assistant radiologist,

" . . . who had only been in the hospital a short time, located the position of a piece of shrapnel which had passed through, and crushed the femur of a man's thigh. The surgeon . . . did not want to probe for the shrapnel from the side from which the radiologist indicated it was accessible;

A marine in France receives first aid before going to a nearby hospital. Marie Curie established X-ray equipment in hospitals only a mile or two from the front.

Marie Curie devoted her time to establishing X-ray facilities during World War I.

instead, he probed from the open wound side. Finding nothing, he decided to explore the region indicated by the radiological examination and immediately extracted the shrapnel."[36]

Irène, who was the "girl assistant radiologist," often found herself in these situations. When she was not quietly forcing older, male doctors to operate where the shrapnel was, she was giving them lessons so they could find the shrapnel on their own.

Working on the
Radium Institute

Marie and Irène spent most of their time from 1915 until the war's end in 1918 setting up and operating X-ray stations. But they still had to get the Radium Institute ready for the day when it would officially open as a center for radiation research. Already, the institute was fulfilling its goal of applying radioactivity to medicine. Bullet wounds and the conditions of life in the trenches produced many candidates eager to try the healing powers of radon gas pellets. Robert Reid wrote that radon "was being used to treat scar tissues, bad cases of arthritis, neuritis [a form of nerve damage] and other assorted ailments."[37] After bringing her gram of radium back from Bordeaux in 1915, Reid said, Marie "began the first French radium therapy service, providing tubes of radon to both civil and military hospitals."[38]

Gradually, Marie, Irène, and the sole remaining lab assistant moved equipment out of Pierre's old lab at the Sorbonne's School of Physics, Chemistry, and Natural History. Marie had never forgiven the university for forcing Pierre to accept the two-room lab as a compromise gesture. In the end, it had been only slightly better than their shed at the School of Industrial Physics and Chemistry. Marie was glad to abandon it for her new laboratories on the street that had been named rue Pierre Curie.

Preparing the institute during wartime was an adventure. For one thing, no one had been available to care for the garden. In 1915, Marie and Irène had to replant the trees and flowers that had been in bloom the previous year. Unfortunately, they chose to do this work just when huge German siege guns, known as Big Berthas, began firing on France from more than twenty miles away. But a year of working near the front had left the Curie women immune to many of the fears of the war.

Frustrations with the Radium Institute

Marie was glad to move into the new Radium Institute and to return to her research after the war. In Pierre Curie, *however, she describes her dissatisfaction with the institute's lack of equipment.*

"This Institute is, however, insufficient in view of the considerable development of radioactivity and of its therapeutic applications. The best authorized persons now recognize that France must possess a Radium Institute comparable to those of England and America for the *Curietherapie* which has become an efficacious [effective] means in the battle against cancer. It is to be hoped that with generous and far-seeing aid, we shall have, in a few years, a Radium Institute complete and enlarged, worthy of our country."

Marie, in a characteristic understatement, noted that she and Irène "spent all that day busy with our plantation, while a few shells fell in the vicinity."[39]

Back to Normalcy

Though Marie, Irène, and many of France's leading scientists survived World War I, many others did not. Marie was personally struck, as Robert Reid reports, by the death of her

> favorite young Polish co-worker, Jan Danysz, who had spent several years of research with her in the Rue Cuvier. He was killed serving as a captain in the artillery. And Rutherford too was grieving over the foolish waste of his brilliant student Harry Moseley, "shot clean through the head" in the Dardanelles campaign. Poland had lost its best French-trained radio-chemist and England the rising star of physics to whom there were few contemporary equals.[40]

Jean Perrin developed an early detection system for aircraft.

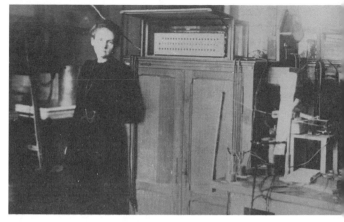

Marie returned to the Radium Institute after the war.

Fortunately, many more scientists were spared when their governments pulled them out of the trenches and had them apply their knowledge to ending the war. One of Marie's colleagues, Jean Perrin, developed a way to detect airplanes by the sound they generated in time to set up anti-aircraft fire. Andre Debierne, the Curies' former assistant who discovered actinium, was the director of France's Chemical Warfare Service. Even Paul Langevin, who had suffered with Marie during the scandal of 1911, was able to help with the early attempts at submarine detection by sonar.

At the end of the war, Marie was faced with having to rebuild much of her staff and to find equipment that her laboratory still needed. The war had drained the finances of both France's government and its citizens. Marie had to beg government officials to let her buy surplus gear at a reduced price for the institute. By 1919, though, both the Curie and the Pasteur branches of the Radium Institute were conducting research with their limited resources. For the next few years, Marie and her staff scraped by with the material they had on hand.

7 Public Relations for Radium

Andrew Carnegie's endowment of the Curies Foundation scholarships had been Marie's first experience with the power her name and her reputation carried. She later used this power to force the University of Paris to build half of the Radium Institute. But until the 1920s, she never thought of using her influence as a way to raise money for new equipment or other research expenses. She did not want to be seen as begging.

The woman who changed Marie's mind about fund-raising was Marie Mattingly Meloney (called Missy by her friends), the editor and star reporter for an American women's magazine, *The Delineator.* Like the famed Madame Curie, Meloney was short, slender, and prone to illnesses that she ignored in pursuit of her work. She was in Europe in the first half of 1920 to write a story on a series of contributions the magazine's publisher had made to victims of the war. She decided that she would combine her trip with a quick visit and interview with Marie.

Assistance from the United States

Because of the Langevin scandal, Marie was still uncomfortable with reporters. Surprisingly, though, she agreed to meet with Meloney. Perhaps Marie had received a good report on the American journalist from a mutual friend who had arranged the meeting. In any case, Meloney arrived at the Radium Institute one day in the summer of 1920. The woman Meloney met was not at all what the journalist expected:

> I remembered that millions of dollars had been spent on radium watches and radium gun sights. Several thousands of dollars' worth of radium was even then stored in various parts of the

Marie Curie grants shipboard interviews on her way to America.

A Pale, Timid Woman

Missy Meloney, in her introduction to Marie's biography, Pierre Curie, *describes her first meeting with Madame Curie.*

"As I entered the new building at Number One Rue Pierre Curie [Pierre Curie Street], which stands out conspicuously among the old walls of the University of Paris, I had already formed a picture of the laboratory of the discoverer of radium.

"I waited a few minutes in the small bare office which might have been furnished from Grand Rapids, Michigan. Then the door opened and I saw a pale, timid little woman in a black cotton dress, with the saddest face I had ever looked upon.

"Her well-formed hands were rough. I noticed a characteristic, nervous little habit of rubbing the tips of her fingers over the pad of her thumb in quick succession. I learned later that working with radium had made them numb. Her kind, patient, beautiful face had the detached expression of a scholar.

"Madame Curie began to talk about America. She had for many years wanted to visit this country, but she could not be separated from her children.

"'America,' she said, 'has about fifty grammes of radium. Four of these are in Baltimore, six in Denver, seven in New York.' She went on naming the location of every grain.

"'And in France?' I asked.

"'My laboratory,' she replied simply, 'has hardly more than a gramme.'

"'*You* have only a gramme?' I exclaimed.

"'I? Oh, I have none,' she corrected. 'It belongs to my laboratory.'

"I suggested royalties on her patents. Surely she had protected her right to the process by which radium is produced. . . . Quietly, and without any seeming consciousness of the tremendous renunciation, she said, 'There were no patents. We were working in the interest of science. Radium was not to enrich anyone. Radium is an element. It belongs to all people.'"

United States. I had been prepared to meet a woman of the world, enriched by her own efforts and established in one of the white palaces of the Champs Elysées or some other beautiful boulevard of Paris.

I found a simple woman, working in an inadequate laboratory and living in an inexpensive apartment, on the meager pay of a French professor.[41]

At that time, Marie's "meager pay" amounted to roughly twelve hundred dollars a month in today's money. This amount was barely enough to pay for the Paris apartment she and her daughters shared, their food, and the occasional trip out of the city. It certainly was not enough for Marie to supplement the institute's small budget. Perhaps the most shocking part of the interview was when Meloney discovered that Marie could not afford to have a larger supply of the element she had discovered:

She had contributed to the progress of science and the relief of human suffering, and yet, in the prime of her life she was without the tools which could enable her to make further contributions of her genius.

At that time the market price of a gramme of radium was one hundred thousand dollars. Madame Curie's laboratory, although practically a new building, was without sufficient equipment; the radium held there was used only for extracting emanations [radon] for hospital use in cancer treatment.[42]

At once, Meloney saw a chance both to benefit the famous scientist and to sell copies of *The Delineator.* If Meloney could raise the money for a gram of radium,

would Marie visit the United States to receive it? At first, Marie hesitated. Despite her years at the Sorbonne, she still had to force herself to stay calm and deliver her lectures. On the trip, she would have to speak in front of thousands of people at various ceremonies.

Worse, an American fund drive could mean the return of reporters prying into her life. The Langevin scandal had received as much publicity in the United States as it had in Europe. Some newspapers in France had defended Marie, but in the United States, the papers focused mainly on her possible guilt. Newspapers across the country still had files filled with information from 1911 they could use to stir up controversy. Marie could not bear the thought of putting herself and her children through that kind of misery again.

Meloney overruled Marie's objections. As editor of *The Delineator,* she had professional and personal contacts at all the important newspapers and press associations. She promised Marie that not even a hint of the old scandal would surface, or at least not in any respected publication. She also convinced Marie that the money and the fame the Radium Institute would gain would outweigh the personal inconvenience of the trip. Marie finally gave in, saying the trip would be a good experience for Irène and Eve.

On her way back to the United States, Meloney began setting up her strategy for the Marie Curie Radium Campaign. Meloney thought she would be able to raise the $100,000 by soliciting a few large donations from wealthy society figures. Marie would quickly receive her gram of radium, and *The Delineator* would be able to feature some of the richest people in the United States in its pages. This plan soon fell through, much to Meloney's surprise. She had been sure these people would want to be associated with the famous scientist. Although she was able to solicit a few large donations, she did not receive enough this way.

However, Meloney knew that Madame Curie was a popular figure with the general public, especially among women. Perhaps, Meloney thought, these people would be willing to help Marie through smaller donations. Many small donations could easily substitute for a few large ones. As a result, the money raised through the radium campaign was a gift to Marie from the mainstream of American society and from the women of the United States in particular.

A Triumphant Visit

It did not take long for Meloney—along with prominent figures like Mrs. John D. Rockefeller and Mrs. Calvin Coolidge, wife of the vice president at the time—to raise the needed money. In fact, when Marie sailed to the United States in early May 1921, the campaign had raised roughly $150,000, which was $50,000 more than what was needed. Meloney increased the surplus when she discovered that the Soviet Union was selling radium at half the going rate.

When Marie arrived in New York, she was immediately swept up in a frenzy of public acclaim. Fortunately, all the publicity her visit generated was positive. Meloney had fulfilled her promise of keeping the 1911 scandal quiet. She had even worked her charm on the managing editor of the *New York Evening Journal,* a leading scandal-seeking paper. In addition to giving Marie a

donation to the fund, Robert Reid claims the editor gave her "his paper's file on the Langevin affair for her to do with what she willed."[43]

The trip itself was a curious combination of success and setbacks. At first, the trip schedule Meloney had arranged seemed reasonable. Over several weeks, Marie would make a few public appearances, attend various awards ceremonies, and tour radium plants. But Meloney had forgotten to allow for Marie's poor health and for the stress each event would create. By the second week of the trip, Marie's arm was in a sling, sprained from the force of hundreds of handshakes. Virtually all of the appearances in the western United States had to be canceled when Marie

Mrs. Calvin Coolidge was a primary organizer of the fund-raiser to buy radium for Marie Curie's laboratory.

nearly collapsed from fatigue. (Marie insisted on seeing the Grand Canyon, however.) Often, Irène or Eve had to substitute for their mother at meetings of professional societies or at university ceremonies.

A Stubborn Streak

The presentation of the gram of radium, which took place in Washington, D.C., had its own small setback. As part of the ceremony, President Warren Harding was to give Marie a deed declaring her to be the owner of the gift of radium. But when Marie saw the deed the night before the

Marie Curie stands next to President Harding at the ceremony where she was given a gram of radium.

President Warren Harding presented Marie with a gift of radium from the United States.

presentation, she declared that it had to be rewritten at once. The radium, she said, *must* be presented as a gift to the Radium Institute, rather than to Marie Curie personally. This seemingly trivial detail unleashed the forceful personality Marie usually kept hidden in public. None of the Marie Curie Radium Campaign officials present could convince the scientist to overlook the discrepancy. Marie was not even willing to wait until morning to alter the document. Despite the lateness of the hour, the campaign officials began searching for a lawyer who would be willing to go to work after most people had gone to bed. Within an hour or two, a new deed had been written that met with Marie's approval. The next day, when President Harding made the presentation, the precious metal became the property of the Radium Institute.

In general, though, the trip was a great success. As Meloney had predicted, Marie gained much more than the promised sample of radium. She also received gifts of other minerals, laboratory equipment, and awards from American professional

In her autobiographical notes to Pierre Curie, *Marie said she had been impressed by the generosity of her hosts during her trip to the United States and by the enthusiasm exhibited by the nation's citizens.*

"The American nation is generous, and always ready to appreciate an action inspired by considerations of general interest. If the discovery of radium has so much sympathy in America, it is not only because of its scientific value, and of the importance of medical utilization; it is also because the discovery has been given to humanity without reservation or material benefits to the discoverers. Our American friends wanted to honor this spirit animating the French science."

and scientific societies totaling almost sixty-nine hundred dollars. A New York publisher gave Marie a check for fifty thousand dollars. The check was an advance payment for her autobiography, which later appeared as part of a biography on Pierre. Of course, Meloney arranged for *The Delineator* to print prepublication excerpts from the book.

Together, the minerals, equipment, and money turned the Radium Institute into a leading laboratory for the study of radioactivity. The trip also revealed to Marie that the life of pure science she had been living since she married Pierre did not have to be one of utter poverty. The very fame she had shunned, the fame that had begun with the award of the 1903 Nobel Prize, could be used to bring in comparatively vast amounts of money for her own research and for that of her colleagues at the Institute. In a very real sense, Marie transformed her fame, which had been created through her scientific work, into another tool of science.

Passing the Reins

After returning from the United States, Marie devised a new role for herself—fund-raiser for the Radium Institute. She now began to accept awards on behalf of the institute. Throughout the 1920s, she devoted much of her time to raising scholarship funds for her students, so they would not have to suffer the same hardships she had. She also made sure they would have the best-equipped laboratories France could supply and would not have to piece experiments together inside old sheds.

Marie raised funds for other groups when she thought it proper. One of her major outside interests was the newly opened Marie Sklodowska-Curie Radium Institute in Warsaw. Poland was busy developing its own scientific base and had decided to honor one of its most famous daughters. But the Polish Radium Institute suffered the same trouble its French counterpart once had—no money for supplies. Though

My Work Is My Life

Marie felt the results of her work justified the hardships she had suffered. In a speech made in 1929 and quoted in the September 1934 issue of Scientific Monthly, *Marie emphasized this belief.*

"President Hoover in making the presentation paid tribute to the fundamental importance of scientific research. Marie Curie in accepting the gift [of radium] said, 'My work is very much my life, and I have been made happy by your generous support of it. . . . I feel deeply the importance of what has been said by the President of the United States about the value of pure science; this has been the creed of my life. Scientific research has its great beauty and its reward in itself; and so I have found happiness in my work.'"

President Herbert Hoover gave Marie a second gift of radium in 1929.

The radium given to Marie Curie by the United States was stored and used in this apparatus.

had earned her doctorate in physics in 1925, with a thesis on the alpha rays emitted by polonium. Naturally, she joined her mother in the institute's Curie Pavilion, as the laboratory building was named. A year later, she married one of Marie's former institute students, Frédéric Joliot. Together, like Marie and Pierre in the 1890s, the Joliot-Curies started work on a series of projects that led them to a Nobel Prize.

As Irène and Frédéric began the research that would lead to their own great discovery—artificial radioactivity—Marie spent less time with the details of running the institute. Gradually, Andre Debierne (who had stayed with Marie ever since the early 1900s) and the Joliot-Curies took over some of these tasks. There were hard feelings against Irène and Frédéric among

President Herbert Hoover with Marie Curie at the Medical Sciences Building in Washington, D.C., where Curie was given money to buy radium for the Radium Institute in her native Poland.

construction started around 1920, by 1928 the institute still did not have any radium.

Marie, a Polish patriot despite her years in France, decided to take part in the institute's fund-raising efforts. With Missy Meloney's help, she made a second and equally successful visit to the United States, though with an easier schedule of events. Once again, she collected enough money to buy laboratory equipment as well as the gram of radium the Polish institute needed.

At the same time, Marie was beginning to hand over the control of the French Radium Institute to her older daughter. Irène

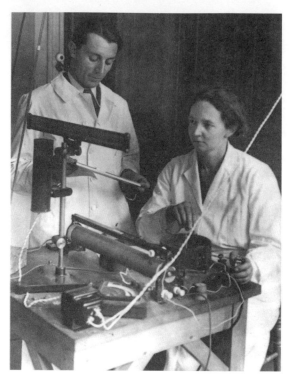

Frédéric and Irène Joliot-Curie in their laboratory in 1934, the year they discovered artificial radiation.

some staff members and outside scientists because Marie had given her daughter and son-in-law preferential treatment when handing out research funds. Critics felt Marie was turning the Curie Pavilion into a family kingdom. And, by marrying Irène, Frédéric was accused of trying to attach himself to the famous name of Curie. However, in the end, the Joliot-Curies did provide a comforting sense of continuity for the institute.

Marie was not able to conduct the same type of ground-breaking research she had done when she was younger. She was not crippled, however. She was able to continue both as director of the Radium Institute and, to a lesser degree, as a research scientist until the 1930s. She also continued to be a stubborn, often difficult person to work with as well as a supportive adviser to her students. But she was beginning to feel the effects of the work that had kept her going for most of her life.

Chapter

8 A Victim of Radiation

Throughout the 1920s, Marie's health seriously deteriorated. At first, her problems were mild. The continual exposure to high levels of radiation had caused cataracts, a clouding of the lens of the eye, to develop in both her eyes. She was operated on a number of times in an attempt to restore her sight, but the cataracts continued to return. Her daughters, her colleagues, and her students went along with Marie's desire to convince the public she was in good health. But even with special glasses, which she wore only in private, she was barely able to read.

Other scientists were also dying of strange diseases that seemed to be connected to their work with radioactivity. Two women, a French chemist known as Madame Artaud and a Polish scientist named Sonia Cotelle, died soon after they accidently spilled radioactive elements on themselves. Two other scientists, Maurice Demenitroux and Marcel Demalander, developed pains and fatigue similar to those Pierre had suffered before his accident. Less than a year after they noticed their ailments, both scientists were dead. Their doctors diagnosed their illnesses as a form of leukemia.

Marie seemed determined not to believe that radium or other radioactive elements were responsible for these deaths.

Perhaps by denying this possibility, she did not have to admit that her life's work was killing her. But available evidence showed that radioactive elements posed potential harm to human beings. Pierre and Henri Becquerel, in fact, had written one of the first papers detailing the burns caused by exposure to radium. Yet a 1925 report by the Curie laboratory on these strange deaths, with Marie's name on it, declared that radium and other elements were not

Radium left painful burns and sores on Marie's fingers and hands.

to blame. It claimed that the minimal precautions common at the time, which included using thin shields of lead and wood, were enough protection for any scientist. According to the report, the deaths were caused by exposure to radioactive gasses trapped in poorly ventilated laboratories.

Marie's apparent denial is even more incredible considering that she and Pierre often warned about the dangers of improperly handling radium. Marie often said that preparing tubes of radon during World War I had left her weakened and prone to illness. Pierre himself was never reluctant to say how dangerous radioactivity was. According to Alex Keller:

> Pierre Curie fancied that radium would provide the light of the future, although he had come painfully to realize the danger involved—to one journalist who asked what he would . . . do with a whole kilo [2.2 pounds] of radium, he replied that it would blind you, burn the skin off your back, and most probably kill you—so, what would he do?—leave the room in a hurry.[44]

The Last Few Years

Despite her denials, Marie's health problems worsened in the 1930s. She had been born with a very sturdy body that could absorb far more punishment than most other people could handle. But she had her limits.

It was a simple stumble at the Radium Institute that showed how badly Marie's body had been damaged. One day in 1932, Marie slipped while walking across her laboratory. She fell on her right arm, breaking her wrist. In itself, the accident was not severe, and her wrist was quickly set in plaster. Even though Marie was sixty-five years old, the injury should have healed within a month.

Instead, Marie became extremely weak and had to be confined to her bed. The radium burns on her fingers, the most visible drawback of her work, became more painful. She began hearing a pounding hum in her head, which made her ears and eyes ache. Kidney and gallbladder disorders, which had plagued her in the past, returned.

Radium's Dangers

Marie Curie warned her colleagues and the public about the danger of radium's power. A profile of Marie published in the July 9, 1921, issue of Scientific American *discussed the issue.*

"Despite twenty years of study and research devoted to radium and radioactivity, Madame Curie admits that she has much to learn. . . . Radium, she tells us, must be handled with great care. Careless or inexperienced handling may prove dangerous and perhaps fatal. We noticed that one of her hands had been affected by the radioactive rays and her general health, so she told us, had been undermined as the result of intensified wartime work with radium."

Marie lectures at the Conservatory of Arts and Techniques shortly before her death in 1934.

True to form, however, Marie went back to work as soon as she was able to do so. She was busy with a number of projects, including writing a textbook on radioactivity and opening the Marie Sklodowska-Curie Radium Institute in Poland. She was also deeply interested in a number of projects her staff and students—Irène and Frédéric, in particular—were working on. Over the next two years, Marie persisted in having a normal, active life, and she continued to ignore her physical ailments.

One of her last moments of pride came in January 1934, when Frédéric and Irène made a great discovery in the field of atomic physics. Using a stream of radium- or polonium-generated particles, they changed a sample of aluminum into a radioactive form of silicon. The Joliot-Curies discovered artificial radioactivity. This discovery earned them the Nobel Prize in physics. Until 1934, the only way to get radioactive material was to buy it from one of the world's limited number of radium plants. Artificial radioactivity lowered the cost of buying such materials overnight

Irène and Frédéric at the Nobel Prize ceremonies in 1935. They received the prize in physics for discovering artificial radiation.

Marie was quietly buried in the Curie's family tomb with her husband, Pierre in 1934.

Although Marie was developing a fever, she went to the clinic at the end of June, accompanied by Eve and a nurse. Marie collapsed before they arrived at their destination. Eve and her nurse rushed Marie to the clinic, where X-ray photographs showed that her lungs were clear. Tuberculosis was not Marie's problem. A blood test showed that both her red and white blood cell counts were far below normal. She was suffering from severe anemia, which is today recognized as a sign of radiation poisoning.

Marie Curie died on July 4, 1934. The day before, her fever had dropped, and she thought the mountain air was beginning to cure her. But her mind began to wander as her body used up the last of its reserves. She alternately complained about her health and confused her hospital room with her laboratory. Eve wrote down her last words: "I can't express myself properly . . . I'd like to put myself straight. My head's turning. . . . Yoghurt: has it been made with radium or mesothorium? . . . I want to be left in peace."[45]

and provided scientists with new radioactive elements. At the same time, though, it caused the collapse of the world's radium extraction industry.

Marie would not witness these developments, however. In the middle of May, Marie was overcome by a fatigue far worse than anything she had felt before. For the rest of May and most of June, she stayed in her Paris apartment while a number of physicians tried to find the cause of her illness. Her doctors finally said her problem was a mild case of tuberculosis, which had killed her mother and her oldest sister. They recommended she spend some time at a health clinic in the mountain town of Sancellemoz located in southeastern France.

Andre Debierne took over this director's office in Marie's laboratory after her death. He carried on her work, and was succeeded by her daughter Irène, and Irène's husband Frédéric.

Irène and Frédéric's work on artificial radioactivity helped scientists develop the first atomic bomb. It was tested in 1945 in Trinity, New Mexico.

Life After Marie

With Irène and Frédéric to take Marie's place, the Radium Institute continued its role as a powerhouse of French atomic physics. Their work on artificial radioactivity had a direct effect on the development of the first atomic bombs in the United States as well as on the development of nuclear power plants. Irène became the third director of the institute's Curie laboratory in 1946, replacing Andre Debierne, who had succeeded Marie. Debierne had been a loyal friend and colleague of Marie's ever since his days as the Curies' lab assistant at the turn of the century. But toward the end of his directorship, he began sharing his duties with Irène.

Marie's death left a profound emptiness in the lives of those who knew her. Even though her colleagues had feared or resented her forceful and often stubborn personality, they had admired her and her achievements. Perhaps one of her most impressive qualities was the way she never became vain as a result of the praise she received in public. Her daughter Eve said that Marie, like Pierre, simply "did not know how to be famous."

Albert Einstein, in a tribute to Marie, said:

> Her strength, her purity of will, her austerity toward herself, her objectivity,

The inside of one of the first nuclear power plants. Artificial radioactivity allowed the kind of research that led to the technology for the plant.

A Servant of Society

Albert Einstein, a professional friend of Marie's, wrote the following tribute to her, which was later published in his 1950 book, Out of My Later Years.

"At a time when a towering personality like Mme. Curie has come to the end of her life, let us not merely rest content with recalling what she has given mankind in the fruits of her work. It is the moral qualities of its leading personalities that are perhaps of even greater significance for a generation and for the course of history than purely intellectual accomplishments. Even these latter are, to a greater degree than is commonly credited, dependent on the stature of character.

"It was my good fortune to be linked with Mme. Curie through twenty years of . . . friendship. I came to admire her human grandeur to an ever growing degree. Her strength, her purity of will, her austerity toward herself, her objectivity, her incorruptible judgment—all these were of a kind seldom found joined in a single individual. She felt herself at every moment to be a servant of society and her profound modesty never left any room for complacency. . . . Once she had recognized a certain way as the right one, she pursued it without compromise and with extreme tenacity.

"The greatest scientific deed of her life—proving the existence of radioactive elements and isolating them—owes its accomplishment not merely to bold intuition but to a devotion . . . under the most extreme hardships imaginable, such as the history of experimental science has not often witnessed."

her incorruptible judgment—all these were of a kind seldom found joined in a single individual. She felt herself at every moment to be a servant of society and her profound modesty never left any room for complacency. . . . Once she had recognized a certain way as the right one, she pursued it without compromise and with extreme tenacity."[46]

Without a doubt, Marie Curie started a revolution in science. When she began her research into the strange phenomenon of Becquerel rays, the atom was one of the great mysteries of nature. Her discoveries of radium and polonium and her investigations of radioactivity helped spur other scientists to find out what was going on inside the atom.

The Trials of a Woman Scientist

The problems women have in gaining acceptance in science have not vanished. An article in the January 27, 1989, issue of Science *relates a story about Lise Meitner, a German atomic physicist.*

"The woman who played a major role in the discovery of fission [Meitner] was once required to work in a converted carpenter's shop with a detached entrance, so as not to fluster her male colleagues. When the British physicist Ernest Rutherford met Lise Meitner . . . for the first time, he exclaimed with astonishment: 'Oh, I thought you were a man.' Meitner spent the rest of Rutherford's visit playing the role of hostess to Mrs. Rutherford."

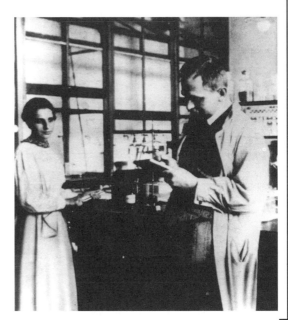

Lise Meitner at work in her laboratory. Male scientists discriminated against her because she was a woman.

Maric's Radium Institute provided research facilities and trained new scientists throughout the century. It was a team of French scientists, led by the Joliot-Curies, that set up France's first atomic reactor after World War II. As France's nuclear industry grew, the country relied on the knowledge of scientists who had been trained or who taught at the institute.

Today, the Radium Institute still conducts research into radioactivity, though it also serves as a museum about Marie Curie and the scientists she worked with.

But Marie's work went beyond stimulating the development of atomic physics. Marie herself became a symbol of science that would inspire women for the rest of the century, even though she never considered

Confusion over Curie's Accomplishments

Despite the fact that Marie Curie is known as a "famous woman scientist," there is a great deal of public confusion over what she is famous for. Even in the year of Marie Curie's death, many people still did not have a clear idea of what she actually had accomplished or how she accomplished it. An obituary in the July 14, 1934, issue of News-Week, *published a week after Marie died, contains examples of this confusion.*

Of course, much of this history is wrong. The truth is that Becquerel, who was actually a physicist, did not discover the activity of uranium until 1896; Marie did not begin investigating uranium until 1898, after she had received her first two degrees from the University of Paris; and she met and married Pierre three years before she began her work on uranium. In addition, in the same article, the magazine claims that "France made her the first woman member of the Academy of Sciences"—a ridiculous error, considering the amount of publicity her failed campaign had generated.

"Almost immediately [after arriving in Paris in 1891] she became interested in a strange phenomenon. In the laboratory of a friend, Becquerel, a French mineralogist, she saw how uranium ore spewed out curious rays that spoiled photographic plates. Marie Curie determined to find out why.

"While at this work she met and married a French physicist 'with auburn hair and large, limpid eyes.' He was Pierre Curie.

"She told him about her work and he decided to help. From their shack laboratory a few days before Christmas, 1898, the discovery of the startling new element, radium, was announced."

Marie and Pierre Curie's work together has often been misreported and misinterpreted.

herself a feminist. She was somewhat pleased when various women's organizations around the world proclaimed her as a champion of women's rights. But first and foremost, she was a scientist, and she wished only to be accepted as such.

In the end, however, Marie Curie became prominent both as a scientist and as a woman. According to biographer Robert Reid:

> Her uniqueness during her creative years lay in the simple fact of her sex. Until the name Marie Curie reached the headlines of popular newspapers there had been no woman who made a significant contribution to science.... As a woman scientist she *was* liberated because she had created the conditions for her own liberation. She had tackled her profession's problems as an equal to all the rest involved; and all the rest happened to be men. She had expected no concessions and none had been made. She had survived because she had made men believe that they were not just dealing with an equal, but with an intensive equal.[47]

Of course, Marie Curie was *not* the first woman scientist or even the first to contribute to scientific knowledge. There were even a number of other women who were struggling for acceptance in their fields at the same time she was. But the importance of Marie Curie lies in the degree of her success. She proved that great discoveries do not come solely from the minds of male scientists like Albert Einstein or her husband, Pierre.

Notes

Introduction: The Accomplishments of Marie Curie

1. Alex Keller, *The Infancy of Atomic Physics: Hercules in His Cradle.* Oxford: Clarendon Press, 1983.

Chapter 1: Polish Childhood, Parisian Scholarship

2. Marie Curie, *Pierre Curie.* Translated by Charlotte & Vernon Kellogg. New York: Macmillan, 1923.

3. Robert Reid, *Marie Curie.* New York: Saturday Review Press/E. P. Dutton, 1974.

4. Marie Curie, *Pierre Curie.*

5. Marie Curie, *Pierre Curie.*

6. Rosalynd Pflaum, *Grand Obsessions: Madame Curie and Her World.* New York: Doubleday, 1989.

Chapter 2: The Discovery of Radium

7. Alex Keller, *The Infancy of Atomic Physics.*

8. Robert Reid, *Marie Curie.*

9. Alex Keller, *The Infancy of Atomic Physics.*

10. Eve Curie, *Madame Curie.* Translated by Vincent Sheean. Garden City, NY: Doubleday, Doran, 1937.

11. Marie Curie, *Pierre Curie.*

12. Marie Curie, *Pierre Curie.*

13. Keith Stewart Thomson, *Living Fossil: The Story of the Coelacanth.* New York: W. W. Norton, 1991.

14. Marie Curie, *Pierre Curie.*

15. Eve Curie, *Madame Curie.*

Chapter 3: Prizes, Poisoning, and Fame

16. Eve Curie, *Madame Curie.*

17. Eve Curie, *Madame Curie.*

18. Marie Curie, *Pierre Curie.*

19. Eve Curie, *Madame Curie.*

20. Eve Curie, *Madame Curie.*

Chapter 4: Heralding the Twentieth Century

21. Alex Keller, *The Infancy of Atomic Physics.*

22. Alex Keller, *The Infancy of Atomic Physics.*

23. Catherine Caufield, *Multiple Exposures: Chronicles of the Radium Age.* New York: Harper & Row, 1989.

24. Catherine Caufield, *Multiple Exposures.*

25. David Wilson, *Rutherford: Simple Genius.* Cambridge: MIT Press, 1983.

26. Catherine Caufield, *Multiple Exposures.*

Chapter 5: Life After Pierre

27. Eve Curie, *Madame Curie.*

28. Eve Curie, *Madame Curie.*

29. Eve Curie, *Madame Curie.*

30. Eve Curie, *Madame Curie.*

31. Marie Curie, *Pierre Curie.*

32. Rosalynd Pflaum, *Grand Obsessions.*

Chapter 6: X Rays at the Front

33. Rosalynd Pflaum, *Grand Obsessions.*

34. Marie Curie, *Pierre Curie.*

35. Marie Curie, *Pierre Curie.*

36. Robert Reid, *Marie Curie.*

37. Robert Reid, *Marie Curie.*

38. Robert Reid, *Marie Curie.*

39. Marie Curie, *Pierre Curie.*

40. Robert Reid, *Marie Curie.*

Chapter 7: Public Relations for Radium

41. Marie Curie, *Pierre Curie.*

42. Marie Curie, *Pierre Curie.*

43. Robert Reid, *Marie Curie.*

Chapter 8: A Victim of Radiation

44. Alex Keller, *The Infancy of Atomic Physics.*

45. Robert Reid, *Marie Curie.*

46. Albert Einstein, "Marie Curie in Memoriam," in *Out of My Later Years.* New York: Philosophical Library, 1950.

47. Robert Reid, *Marie Curie.*

For Further Reading

Norv Brasch, "Cradle of the Nuclear Age (Explorations)," *Omni,* March 1981.

Eve Curie, *Madame Curie.* Translated by Vincent Sheean. Garden City, NY: Doubleday, Doran, 1937.

David W. Lillie, *Our Radiant World.* Ames: Iowa State University Press, 1986.

Vera Rubin, "Women's Work," *Science 86,* July/August 1986.

Tom Valeo, "Luminous Lessons," *Chicago* magazine, December 1984.

Works Consulted

Catherine Caufield, *Multiple Exposures: Chronicles of the Radium Age.* New York: Harper & Row, 1989.

Marie Curie, *Pierre Curie.* Translated by Charlotte & Vernon Kellogg. New York: Macmillan, 1923.

Marie Curie, *Radioactive Substances.* Translator unknown. New York: Philosophical Library, 1961.

Albert Einstein, *Out of My Later Years.* New York: Philosophical Library, 1950.

Timothy Ferris, *The World Treasury of Physics, Astronomy, and Mathematics.* Boston: Little, Brown, 1991.

Woods Hutchinson, *The Doctor in War.* Boston: Houghton Mifflin Company, 1918.

Alex Keller, *The Infancy of Atomic Physics: Hercules in His Cradle.* Oxford: Clarendon Press, 1983.

Edward R. Landa, "The First Nuclear Industry," *Scientific American,* November 1982.

Austin C. Lescarboura, "A Chat with Madame Curie," *Scientific American,* July 9, 1921.

Alan P. Lightman, "To Cleave an Atom," *Science 84,* November 1984.

Marilyn Bailey Ogilvie, *Women in Science: Antiquity Through the Nineteenth Century.* Cambridge, Mass.: The MIT Press, 1986.

Rosalynd Pflaum, *Grand Obsession: Madame Curie and Her World.* New York: Doubleday, 1989.

Robert Reid, *Marie Curie.* New York: Saturday Review Press/E. P. Dutton, 1974.

E. (Ernest) Rutherford, *Radio-Activity.* Cambridge: Cambridge University Press, 1905.

Londa Schiebinger, *The Mind Has No Sex?: Women in the Origins of Modern Science.* Cambridge: Harvard University Press, 1989.

Keith Stewart Thomson, *Living Fossil: The Story of the Coelacanth.* New York: W. W. Norton, 1991.

David Wilson, *Rutherford: Simple Genius.* Cambridge: MIT Press, 1983.

Index

Picture Credits

American Institute of Physics Niels Bohr Library, 27 (top), 33, 45 (top), 60, 66 (bottom)

AP/Wide World Photos, 26 (top), 65 (bottom), 79 (bottom), 87 (bottom)

Archives P. et M. Curie, Paris, 15 (bottom), 27 (bottom), 28, 34, 35 (both), 36 (both), 37, 39, 44, 56, 58 (bottom), 59, 74, 88, 91 (bottom), 92 (both)

The Bettmann Archive, 8, 9 (bottom), 11, 12, 14, 15 (top), 16, 17, 18, 21, 24 (bottom), 25 (both), 26 (bottom), 30, 40, 41, 42, 47, 48 (top), 50, 53, 58 (top), 62, 64 (both), 65 (top), 66 (top), 67, 70 (both), 73, 77 (bottom), 79 (top), 83, 91 (top), 93 (bottom), 96

Carnegie Library, Pittsburgh, 61

Culver Pictures, Inc., cover, 13, 57, 63, 71 (bottom), 80

Otto Hahn: A Scientific Autobiography. NY: Charles Scribner's Sons, 1966, 95

Historical Pictures, 9 (top)

Library of Congress, 7, 20, 23, 86, 89

National Archives, 71 (top), 76, 77 (top), 93 (top)

National Center for Atmospheric Research, 24 (top)

James Stevenson/Science Photo Library, 45 (bottom)

UPI/Bettmann, 29, 48 (bottom), 51, 55, 69, 84 (both)

UPI/Bettmann Newsphotos, 87 (top)

About the Author

Originally a physics major, free-lance writer Sean Grady received a Bachelor of Arts degree in print journalism from the University of Southern California in 1988. While in college, he worked for the entertainment section of the *Los Angeles Times* as a reporting intern; for *California Magazine* as a research intern; and for the City News Service of Los Angeles, a local news wire, as a general assignment reporter. In the two years after his graduation, Grady specialized in business reporting and worked as business editor of *The Olympian,* a daily newspaper in Olympia, Washington. Grady currently lives in Sparks, Nevada.